TAPADERO

The Making of a Cowboy

NUMBER **11**
THE M. K. BROWN RANGE LIFE SERIES

TAPADERO

THE MAKING OF A COWBOY

by WILLIE NEWBURY LEWIS

FOREWORD BY VICTOR WHITE

UNIVERSITY OF TEXAS PRESS : AUSTIN & LONDON

Library of Congress Cataloging in Publication Data

Lewis, Willie Newbury.
    Tapadero: the making of a cowboy.

    (The M.K. Brown range life series, no. 11)
    1. Lewis, William J., 1870–1960. 2. Ranch life
—Texas. 3. Cattle trade—Texas. I. Title.
F391.L482L4   917.64'8 [B]   76–185237
ISBN 0-292-78001-X

© 1972 by Willie Newbury Lewis

All rights reserved

Composition and presswork by
The University of Texas Printing Division, Austin

Bound by Universal Bookbindery, Inc., San Antonio

To the memory of my son William, in whose heart lay a deep and lasting love of the Panhandle prairies and plains.

CONTENTS

Foreword xi

Preface xv

The Making of a Cowboy 3

Index 185

ILLUSTRATIONS

Following page 112

1. Charles Lewis
2. Hallie Koogle Lewis
3. The Lewis Home in Frederick
4. William, at Ten
5. William, at Twenty-two
6. William J. Lewis at Seventy-five
7. Carrie Koogle
8. Sheriff Al Gentry
9. The Rowe Brothers

Map of the Panhandle, p. 4

FOREWORD

Violence is the word that comes to mind when one thinks of the Texas frontier, especially up north in the Panhandle in the 1880's. Everything was extreme: the vast horizon-to-horizon prairies broken only by sprawling, endlessly winding draws; the climate, which clamped down on the land with paralyzing blizzards in the winter, abounded in hailstorms and cloudbursts that turned the parched draws into raging torrents in a matter of minutes in the summer, and caught the unwary newcomer with its northers—the sudden chilling winds that could drop the temperature by thirty degrees in less than half an hour—on what had been a pleasant autumn afternoon. And there were the men: they were most extreme of all and had the seeds of violence in them.

It is a pleasant fiction, part of American mythology, that the frontier drew the strong, the courageous, the adventuresome. It did, but it also drew the weak—the men who had failed in the East or the South, who were having another go at it and sometimes made it, but who just as often failed again and became desperate and, with the false courage of the six-shooter in the hand, were ready tools for the irresponsible. As for the strong, it depends what kind of strength is meant. To be sure, there were men of courage and integrity, men with modest ambitions and stubborn memories of a well-ordered existence they had left behind and wanted to recreate on the frontier; but for the most part the strength of the strong men was lined with ruthlessness bred of greed and a lust for power. In a land where there was little, if any, law, such men were like balloons in a vacuum: their ambitions were free to expand. Any obstacle in their path was promptly crushed. Only the fact that there were other strong men around provided a check—that, and nature. If, on the one hand, the strong man's greed and the endless expanse of free grass land invited him to put out great herds of cattle in the attempt to make millions in a couple of years, there were the winter freezes that could turn half his cattle into stiff-frozen mockery of his ambitions, and the droughts that made cattle waste away for lack of grass and water. That was another form of violence, and it made the strong men even more ruthless and determined.

That in such a rough and tough world a mere boy from Maryland, who hardly knew a calf from a deer and who had never been on a horse, should gradually but steadily make his way and, as a comparatively young man, end up with one of the great ranches in the Panhandle is little short of the marvelous—and to that extent, at least, in keeping with this country of extremes. It happened.

Early in the 1880's fifteen-year-old William J. Lewis came out from Maryland with his parents, who had been talked into investing in a ranch by a relative intoxicated with golden visions of a fortune to be made in a few years. One hundred and fifty thousand dollars was money in the 1880's, and the three partners promptly lost it to a freeze and two droughts and the shiftlessness of the entrepreneur partner. It looked as if everything had been lost, except the integrity of the young man's father, who insisted on paying off every cent of debt on the ranch if it took the rest of his life—and except for the curious fact that young William J. Lewis had fallen in love with the prairies and cattle and horses the moment he had arrived in Clarendon. Unlike his uncle, whose only ambition had been millions, William had only one ambition: to make himself into a first-rate cowboy.

Mrs. Lewis tells the story of that apprenticeship by the man she married and who was twenty-one years older than herself with modesty and a minimum of rhetoric. The story did not need that; it was rich enough in itself and contains the material for half a dozen synthetic westerns. For there were unusual difficulties in the way of a well-bred boy from the East. Not the least one was a 115-pound ranch foreman, a bundle of guts and competence and authority, who felt offended by the boy's apparent gentleness and was determined to break the boss's kid. Mrs. Lewis presents as exciting a hellion as can be found anywhere in fiction in this same Red, who makes the young William stand night watches over the horses against Indian horse thieves when the boy has to start helping the cook get breakfast long before sunup, who assigns him the meanest bronc as his horse, who makes him crawl into a cave in the canyon wall to rope a she-wolf with her young.

It is only the beginning of that apprenticeship, for presently there were the cattle rustlers, the nesters, and the gunmen to worry about, and, above all, the cattle barons like Goodnight who could spot competition immediately and who lost no time in trying to get rid of it. Mrs. Lewis shows how the polite young man from Maryland apposed his own brand of strength to the violence of the Panhandle—a stubborn Sunday-school kind of nonviolence, backed by courage instead of guns. In a country where the six-shooter was in every man's hand, he refused to wear a gun; where swearing was part of the *lingua franca*, he never swore; where no man would get on a horse without wearing high-heeled cowboy boots—to keep the foot from slipping through a stirrup and being dragged when a horse panicked and ran away—he wore low-heeled shoes and liked the Mexican *tapadero*, the slipper-like leather guard over the front of the stirrup, to avoid the risk of being dragged. It was almost as if he wanted to assert his aloofness from the West, while at the same time he loved the land, the cattle, the horses, and the people who echoed the decencies of the East, the comeliness of the life his parents stood for. It was independence, too, but novel, not the usual kind of Texas independence.

Yet at the time a boy nowadays is about a junior in college, he was top hand—about the equivalent of a colonel in the army—of the big R. O. Ranch; at thirty he was already a highly regarded cattleman who could lease a ranch of over half a million acres; and shortly thereafter he became owner of the famous R. O. Ranch he had always dreamed about.

Straight Horatio Alger, except that the subject of Mrs. Lewis' biography did not marry the boss's daughter: he made it on his own. Pure Texas, but a Texas that Texans like to think about on Sundays by the poolside, a Texas without benefit of oil wells and scabrous incidents that they prefer to forget. It is the Texas that grand historian of the cowboy, Frank Dobie, loved.

VICTOR WHITE

PREFACE

My husband, William J. Lewis, moved with his parents, Hallie Koogle and Charles Lewis, to the Texas Panhandle during the eventful period when the eras of buffalo hunting, Indian subjugation, free grass, and barbed wire were being telescoped into the short span of twenty-five years. His experiences as the family made the difficult adjustment to a new way of life and as he slowly, day by day, acquired the art of being a cowboy are typical of the character of those who shaped the West. Realizing that his story was also the story of the Panhandle and that the one could not be told accurately without familiarity with the other, I set out to increase my source material by collecting the reminiscences of every available early settler. I ended by interviewing forty-eight old-timers. Among the more important were Morris Rosenfield, the Rosie of the present story; T. D. Hobart, who was connected with the New York and Texas Land Company as early as 1882 and was also coexecutor with Mr. Henry Coke of the J. A. Ranch after Mrs. Adair's death; Mrs. Olive King Dixon, whose husband fought in the Battle of Adobe Walls; and Mrs. Bertha Doan Ross, whose family established Doan's Crossing on Red River. The interviews were taken during the early half of the 1930's.

It was never my intention to write a simple biography of my husband, but rather to record for permanence, by means of his experiences and the people and places he knew, a historically accurate account of the colorful era of the 1880's.

If I have succeeded in my purpose, it is largely through the assistance of Mr. Victor White; his corrections, suggestions, and additions contributed much toward giving the manuscript publishable form.

TAPADERO

The Making of a Cowboy

CHAPTER I

Extending northward above the central body of Texas is a wide stretch of prairie and plain, known as the Panhandle. Its western half is a high, broad, slanting tableland fringed on the east by the breaks—the ridges and canyons of the escarpment—which lead to the prairies below. Cutting a gorge across this tableland is the Canadian River. To the south, two forks of the Red River bisect the prairie lands: the Salt Fork and the Prairie Dog Fork, which runs through the Palo Duro Canyon and then turns right to form the region's southern boundary. To the west is New Mexico; to the east, Oklahoma, originally named the Indian Territory. The plains and prairies together form a semiarid grassland where blizzards, heat, cloudbursts, drought, tornadoes, hailstorms, dust, and wind are common occurrences.

In 1876 Charles Goodnight moved from Colorado to place his initial herd of cattle on the grass beside the Palo Duro Canyon. Two years later Lewis Henry Carhart, a minister from Sherman, Texas, came both to establish the Quarter Circle Heart Ranch and to find a suitable settlement for a group of Methodist followers. He placed his settlement in the center of the ranch on a high bluff above the Salt Fork and gave it the dignified name of the Christian Colony of Clarendon.

The year was 1885. It was late spring. A slightly built, towheaded boy of fourteen[1] stepped down from the chair car in which he and the other members of his family had made the final stage of their journey from Maryland to Fort Worth. Failing to notice that his

---

[1] William turned fifteen shortly after he arrived in Texas.

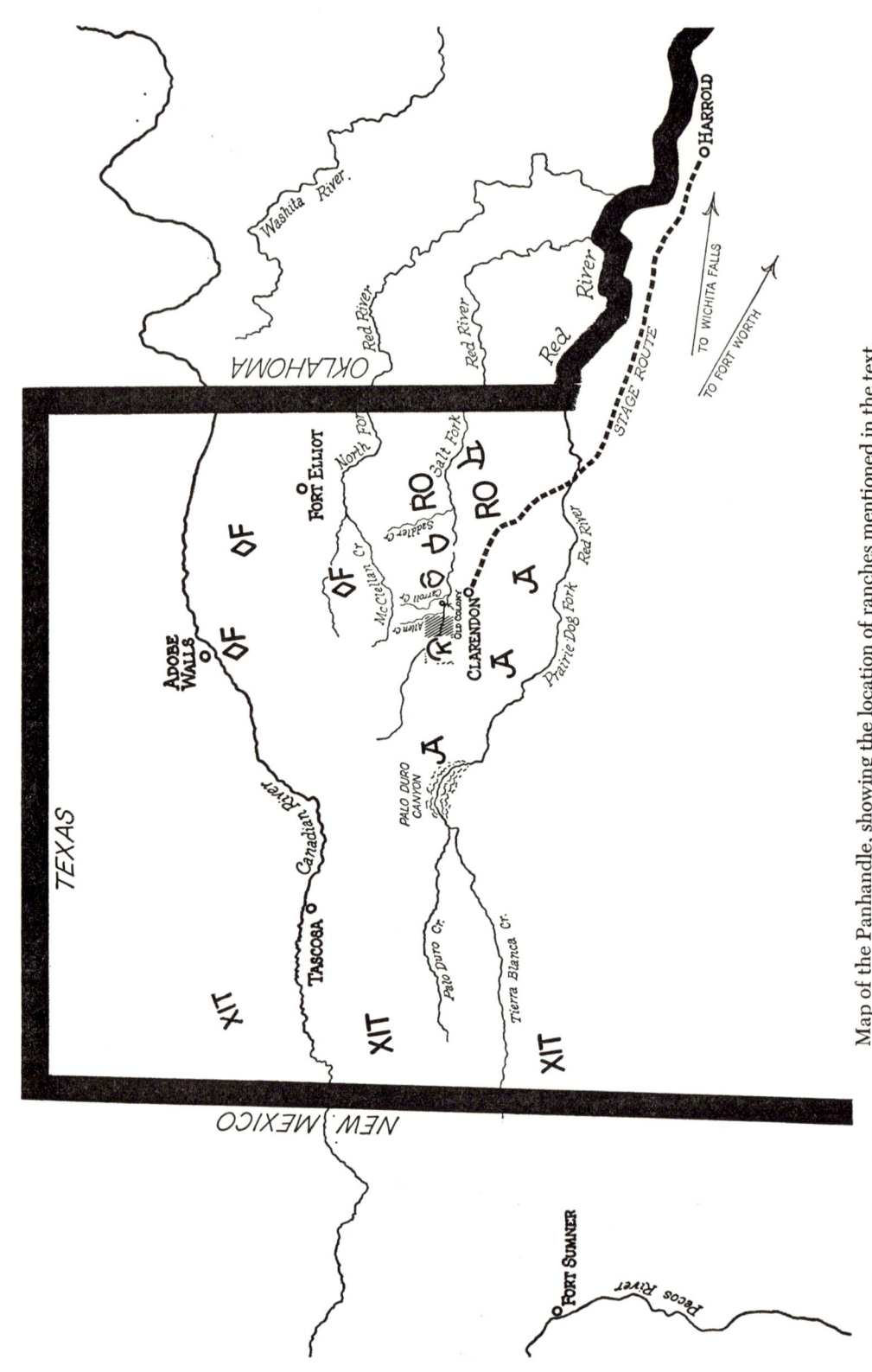

Map of the Panhandle, showing the location of ranches mentioned in the text.

mother, father, and sister Katie,[2] after getting off the train, had stopped where the luggage was being placed, he walked on, glancing from side to side as if in search of something.

"Wait, William," his father called in the unauthoritative voice of a man of small stature. "I know how eager you are about everything, but the other train is ready to start. It's waiting there on the next track. The important thing right now is to get ourselves and our belongings over there and settled."

The boy turned quickly and retraced his steps. From the piled-up bags, boxes, and parcels, he chose a makeshift cage in which huddled two unhappy pigeons. After settling the cage in the crook of one arm, he picked up, with his free hand, a large, cloth-covered suitcase and, with some difficulty, started in the direction indicated.

When he was close to the train, he noticed it was very different from the trains he had been on so far. It had no passenger cars but was made up of a long line of flatcars stacked with lumber and one boxcar through the boarded-up door of which he glimpsed the heads of horses and cows and the wrinkled face of an old woman with her head tied in a scarf. Behind the boxcar was the caboose, in which passengers were evidently to ride. After a second trip back and forth, he had all the luggage aboard.

The train started with a jerk. As dictated by the rise and fall of the land, it moved steadily upward toward higher country. When the big red wheels turned fast, the cars rocked and bumped over the unsettled roadbed, and black cinder-filled smoke poured from an oversized smokestack.

There were no passengers other than the Lewis family, and William settled down with his face at the window, hoping to discover something of more interest than the tracks and railroad workers behind the Fort Worth station. At some distance on the side, he had noticed cattle pens, but, to his disappointment, no cattle were visible.

As the train moved away from town, small groves of post oak could

---

[2] There was a younger brother, Charles, familiarly known as Tod. He will never be mentioned because he plays no part in the story. Tod did not come with his parents to Texas but remained behind to continue his schooling. Later he attended school for two years in Fort Worth after which he returned to Washington, D.C., where he settled permanently.

be seen. Spring was not yet over, and the earth was still carpeted with green. Wildflowers grew in profusion: yellow buttercups, red Indian blanket, and wild verbena. Every so often tiny funnels of wind and sand arose from nowhere to whirl madly across the landscape.

The boy watched for a while, then put his head back and closed his eyes. Maybe Texas was not going to be as much fun as he had expected after all. He wondered what his playmates, Bernie and Grant, back in Maryland were doing. Tomorrow would be Saturday, and, if it were a warm day, they would spend it on the Monocacy— swimming in the river, picnicking by the water's edge, and hunting birds' eggs in the many trees that grew along the bank. Maybe in Texas he could find some eggs he had never seen before. At this point he was brought back to the present by the voice of the conductor announcing their arrival in Wichita Falls. The hotelkeeper's beckoning gestures, accompanied by a clanging bell, informed the passengers that a hot dinner awaited them at the hotel across the street.

Wichita Falls marked the beginning of the plains. There were no trees except those indicating the presence of a creek, but the shrublike mesquite with its lacy foliage and unfilled bean pods was everywhere. Soon the prairies began to flatten out.

In the late afternoon the train reached Harrold. A railroad town in its most primitive stage, it was unlike anything William had ever seen before. Although the track extended some distance up the line, this was the last town. Tents littered the landscape. The only wooden structures were the hotel, the saloon, and the cattle pens. On a siding stood the temporary station, a red boxcar with H-A-R-R-O-L-D painted in bold white letters across one side.

A plank walk led directly from the track across a wide dirt expanse to the hotel. In the open space in between, most of the town's male population stood waiting for the train's arrival. A little to one side of the others, a group of three youngsters sat in a squatting position on the high heels of their ornate boots. Except for a difference in the color of their outfits, they were dressed alike: in doeskin pants, bright shirts, and brighter neckerchiefs. On their heads were wide-brimmed felt hats. At the sight of William's parents and sister, the three boys rose to their feet, and, like the other bystanders, stood, hat in hand, until the newcomers passed through the hotel door.

William, with the bird cage in his arm, was still standing by the train looking around when his attention was caught by the youngsters. Hitched to a rail close by them were three ponies. Cowboys! he thought, as he started across the road. But his excitement was not long-lived. Suddenly, he was conscious of his own contrasting appearance, and for the first time in his life, he felt resentment toward his mother. She should have known that Texas boys of his age did not wear knickerbockers, long black stockings, ruffled shirts, and sailor hats with ribbon streamers. He had never before felt so humiliated.

As if to comfort him in his misery, the gentler of the two pigeons began to coo, at which a thought flashed across his mind. Hastily he opened the door of the cage, pulled the bird out, and turned it loose. Up it flew for some fifteen or twenty feet, then, after circling once, came back to him, to settle contentedly on his shoulder. By this time he had almost reached the bystanders. With pretended unconcern, he put the bird back in the cage, fastened the cage door, and walked past them into the hotel.

As William's father approached the desk to register, his mother said, "Please do not separate us. I shall feel much better tonight if we are all together in one room."

The hotelkeeper laughed and responded, "The rooms are mighty small for the four of you." But William's mother remained firm, adding, "I prefer being crowded to being uneasy."

It was not until they reached the second floor that they noticed the shoddy construction of the building in which they were to spend the night. The hall was long and narrow, with doors at regular intervals, indicating a series of rooms. The floor and the outside walls were of only one-plank thickness, and the partitions between the rooms did not reach the ceiling. The bedrooms were all the same—crude and cramped, with two cots, a rocking chair, and a table on which stood a basin and a pitcher of water with a slop-jar underneath. There was no bed.

After throwing herself into the chair, William's mother pointed to the jar and said, "I don't want to resort to that 'til I have to. Please, one of you, go downstairs and find out where the toilets are."

"I'll go," William said, and rushed out of the room. On finding the lobby empty, he went outside, prepared to accost the first person he encountered.

"Excuse me, sir," he said to an old man near the entrance. "My mother sent me downstairs to find the toilet for her. Can you tell me where it is?"

The stranger looked puzzled and shook his head. After a moment, however, his expression changed, and, with his face in a broad smile, he slapped William on the back and replied, "The privies? Is that what you mean? Why didn't you say so in the first place? You'll find 'em around the corner."

With an embarrassed "Thank you," William turned and walked to the back. A sandy plain, unbroken by trees, extended as far as he could see. A short distance from the hotel ten or fifteen tents had been pitched. In the space in between were two loosely thrown together outhouses, the one marked "Ladies," the other "Gents." Mother won't like this, he thought, as he walked back upstairs.

After an early supper they went directly to bed, in preparation for the long, difficult day that was to follow. The others in the family were soon asleep, but not William. There was too much excitement in this strange, new world to which he had come. In the absence of a lock, his cot, as a safety measure, had been placed across the door. As he tossed about to get comfortable, he noticed a narrow beam of light coming up from the floor. He realized after a second that it came from a knothole in one of the floor planks and that, if the hole were large enough, he might be able to see through it. As quietly as possible, for it would spoil everything if he aroused his parents, he slipped from the cot to the floor. With one eye pressed tightly against the opening, he found he was able to see almost all of the room below.

It was the hotel dining room. Already the supper tables had been cleared; at the center table the hotelkeeper was dealing cards. Seated around him were some older men and three train crewmen in an early stage of inebriation.

After a while the gamblers were joined by another player, tall, well-built, and blond. The dark blue of his high-buttoned coat became his erect figure and open face well, as did the trousers with the wide gold stripe. On his sleeves were the chevrons of a sergeant. He stopped at the first table he passed to lay his carbine and dragoon pistol down. Next, he removed his coat and, after folding it carefully, placed it by the side of his firearms. Having made himself comfortable, he sat down to play. "He's a soldier," William thought, "from the fort that is near the place where we are going to live."

It was the first time the boy had watched men gambling. It added to the excitement to see that the game was not being played as a game; gambling was serious business. He lay for a long time without moving, with first one eye, and, then, the other, tight against the little hole in the floor. Gradually, on the table in the room below, the many greenback and silver dollars, which had changed hands often during the evening, lay in two piles: one in front of the soldier, and the other in front of the hotelkeeper. It was long after midnight when his mother wakened and firmly ordered him back to bed.

Morning came much too fast for him. By five o'clock—he had difficulty keeping his eyes open—William and his family were seated at the table, which only the instant before, it seemed to him, had been covered with poker chips and money.

To the waitress's question, "Do you want your eggs straight up or turned over," he replied, "I'll have one of each kind, please."

"Son," his mother began. "You—"

"I know I am not really that hungry. But, mother, it was the only way I could find out what she meant. If I'm going to live in Texas, I want to know what people are talking about."

CHAPTER II

Soon after breakfast, they were on their way. Their destination, the colony of Clarendon, lay 150 or more miles to the northwest. Although the drive was to be continuous, with stops only to water and change the teams, it would require all of one day and night, and part of a second morning. Coffee and food were said to be available at some of the stage stations, but William's father, at the hotelkeeper's suggestion, ordered a lunch to take along for his family.

The conveyance in which they were to ride was waiting when they stepped through the hotel door. To William's surprise, it bore no resemblance to the overland stage of which he had seen pictures. It was not a stage but a "jerky"—a sort of three-seated hack or wagon, with the body swung on leather straps to ease its sudden and sometimes violent movements. There was a canvas top, but the sides were open, an arrangement that left the passengers at the mercy of the spring sun and wind. A few pieces of baggage were tied on top, and the mail bag was attached to a boot suspended out the back. The four animals hitched to the stage were snorting and pawing at the ground.

"Don't pay no 'tention to them old Spanish mules," the driver said when he saw William's mother hesitate. "Jist git in and git settled. They caint git away till their bridles is turned loose. Even then they caint do much till the wheels on the right side is untied; and we aint gonna do that till after them fiery animals has run far enough to let off a lot of their steam. Put the boy up here in front with me."

Once released, the mules dashed away with as much speed as possible under their handicap, across the track, and out onto the prairie. As the driver had predicted, it was not long before they settled down into an easy gallop, a pace they maintained until reaching the next stage stand where fresh mules were put in their place.

After Pease River was crossed, there was a decided change in the atmosphere. The air seemed more invigorating. The prairies were no longer level but rose and fell in huge ground swells, and the face of the country became harsh and stark in its beauty.

As the top of one rise was reached, the stagedriver, whose name turned out to be Satterwhite, pointed to the west. "There aint nothin' particular to see, but look anyway. That smoky cloud hanging just above the land is about thirty miles away. You can sure see a long way off in the Panhandle."

After giving William time to look, he turned and said, "Are your folks plannin' to stay in Clarendon?"

"Yes, sir."

"Well, do tell. I run a livery stable there. You're gonna like livin' in this part of the world. I've been here a long time. I remember the day we decided to leave Kansas and follow the buffalo west. That was the move that cost me my hand. Funny thing—it aint slowed me down none. I git along jest as good with this here thing," he said and raised up the hook that protruded from his left sleeve.

"I have an uncle," William said, "who was a buffalo hunter in Kansas and came out here after the buffalo, just like you. Maybe you know Uncle Bill. Bill Koogle's his name."

"You don't mean to say old Bill, the bullwhacker, is kin to you? We used to drive freight wagons together, but the last I heard of him he had gone out to fence Goodnight's place. Well, I'll declare."

"I don't know what a bullwhacker is, but my mother—he's my mother's brother—says that since he left Gettysburg College, he's tried about everything. He was only seventeen when he ran away."

All through lunch, which he proudly shared with his new friend, and on through the afternoon the stories continued. William sat spellbound as he listened to tales of the first Indian raid at Doan's Crossing, of the peaceful Kiowa that roamed up and down Red River, of Quanah Parker and his warring Comanches, and to a whole list of names never heard of in Maryland.

Toward the end of the afternoon Satterwhite said, "You're a smart kid. If you can learn to swing onto them mules and to tie and untie them wheels fast enough, I might think about puttin' you on a stage run."

"Thank you, sir," William replied, not sure whether he was taking the compliment too seriously. "I'd like any kind of job around horses, but these aren't exactly horses. Anyway, I want to be a cowboy. Can you teach me to be a cowboy?"

"No, son. I caint teach you that, and neither can nobody else. You have to do it all by yourself. First you'll start out doin' all the dirty jobs, like pullin' cattle out of bog holes and diggin' post holes for this new barbed wire ever'body's so taken with; and if you never ask questions, never ask help, and never complain, but jist keep on workin' good, maybe, one day the foreman will put you on a horse. The ridin' and ropin' aint so hard. Most anybody can kinda learn to do it. But the fello' that does it good does it because he's got somethin' in here the others aint—a sort of feel that tells you what to do and when. If you've got it, you'll jist go on till one morning you'll wake up to find out you're a cowboy.

"But," he went on, "there's one thing you gotta do and fast—that's change your name. I aint never heard tell of a cowboy called William."

As the old man talked, the jerky swayed and bounced its way across the prairie ruts and arroyos. It was late afternoon before the teams were brought to a stop by the side of a small creek. The stage stand was close by. William jumped out to wash in the cool waters. While the mules were being harnessed, he helped his mother and Katie spread supper under the tall cottonwoods that grew along the bank. Because of the pleasure everyone took in the water and shade, the dried-out food became unimportant.

Soon dusk closed in, and the night ride began. Satterwhite seemed to have talked himself out, and William was beginning to feel sleepy. He had just started to doze when the clatter of the approaching downstage aroused him. With some misgivings, he remembered that their Cousin Em's husband, Ralph Jefferson, was planning to meet his parents at this point, in order to ride back into Clarendon with them. At the sound of the wheels there flashed through William's mind a conversation he had overheard last winter. His mother was talking to his father. "Poor Em," she had said, "her father-in-law, I am certain, has persuaded her to uproot herself, to take Harry out of Georgetown University, and to move to Texas in the hope that the simple life of the frontier and the separation from the convivial society of Washington would induce her husband to start leading a more responsible life."

If there were a change in Ralph, it was not easily discernible. There he was, beruffled shirt and all—"the perfect dandy" as William's father called him.

William stirred uneasily; the remainder of the trip was spoiled for him, and he knew it. He was never comfortable in Ralph's presence. Furthermore, he was embarrassed that his new friend, Satterwhite, should see his relative, even though only a second cousin by marriage, in clothes so unsuited to those around him.

His parents rushed over to greet their cousin, but William did not join them. After delaying as long as he dared without attracting his mother's notice, he got out, walked over to Ralph, shook his hand, and, without further ado, returned to his seat beside Satterwhite. Neither he nor the driver had much to say as the stage bounded along through the night. It was past midnight when they reached Rustler's Creek, the last stop before crossing the river. Against the creek's opposite bank, but on a flat high enough to offer protection against a rise, as Satterwhite called it, could be seen the outline of the stagekeeper's dugout.

After repeated "Hello's" from Satterwhite, a man appeared. His face was heavily creased and tanned, and on his chin grew the reddish stubble of several shaveless days. In his hand he carried a basin of grease, from the side of which hung a twist of burning rag. A disheveled woman and several dirty, half-naked children followed shyly behind him. Despite his appearance, he came forward to greet the passengers pleasantly and with ease. On seeing the two women, he offered them the loan of his bed, if they cared to rest until the next day's stage. William's mother made her refusal as courteous as the stagekeeper's invitation.

For the first time in several hours William was amused. He had never before thought of his mother except in the two-story house above the store in Maryland, with big, fat Dinah to cook for her and young Mary to do the other chores. To imagine her lying on a filthy pallet in a dugout made him smile.

The river was twenty miles farther on. A long hill led down to the river basin. A small, shallow stream was all that was visible.

"We calls this the Red," Satterwhite explained, "but it aint really. It's just the Prairie Dog Fork, and it has to travel a long way, clear to the Indian Territory border before it gits to the real stream. It don't look like much now, but you oughta see it sometime during a rise. It spreads out for a quarter of a mile."

Cedar-dotted mounds were scattered along the bank, and the moonlight, which shone strong and bright, added an eerie quality to the scene.

After another stop at Buck Creek for breakfast, they were on the final stage of their journey. At the foot of the hill lay a small lake. As they made their approach toward the Salt Fork, the driver, of necessity, turned abruptly away from the river to avoid making an uphill pull that would have been difficult with a heavy load; then he continued down the winding draw that led to Kelly Creek. Once beyond the creek, the road ran along the river for a mile, then turned at right angles to cross to the north bank.

There, on a slightly elevated flat near the place where Carroll Creek and the Salt Fork came together, nestled the colony of Clarendon. For the first time, William saw the town that was to become his future home. He could hardly contain his excitement.

CHAPTER III

Three years before William and his family reached Clarendon, his mother's brother, Bill Koogle, had gone on a honeymoon trip with his bride, Carrie, to Maryland. While visiting his relatives there, Koogle persuaded William's father[1] and Ralph Jefferson to become his partners in the establishment of a free grass Panhandle ranch, which he would operate. To form the initial capital each partner put in $50,000 in cash. With this $150,000, Bill was to purchase land, cattle, horses, and equipment, to build headquarters for the outfit, and to do whatever fencing was necessary.

Bill's first step after his return to Texas was to buy the Sacra and Sugg Ranch, which was some eighteen miles to the northwest of Clarendon. It was ideal ranch country. Its location below the cap rock gave it protection against the strong winds and bitter temperatures that prevailed on the Great Plains in winter and made it an excellent range for cows. It was also land through which numerous

---

[1] There were several others who invested small amounts—probably William's grandfather and his mother's sisters.

creeks ran—Allen, Record, Rawhide, and Boggy, where many of the new ranch's cattle were to die in future years. Living water was highly prized by all stockmen. Furthermore, the nucleus of the Sacra and Sugg property had been made through the purchase of the Franklin school block, which gave the ranch the advantage of possessing at least twenty sections in one solid tract about two miles wide and twelve miles long.

The J. A. Ranch, which belonged to Charles Goodnight and John Adair,[2] formed the ranch's southern boundary; the Quarter Circle Heart, its eastern; and the Diamond F,[3] a part of its northern. To the west extended the free grass of a vast open range, as yet unsurveyed. Adjoining the Diamond F was the area through which McClelland Creek and its subsidiaries ran. Although not a part of the Sacra and Sugg property by purchase, it was claimed through the squatter's rights of the former ranchowners, who had occupied it from the day they bought the Franklin school block. When Koogle built his west fence, he did not hesitate to extend it straight to the Diamond F, making a rectangle that enclosed not only the McClelland meadow, as the part where the tallest grasses grew was called, but every school section lying between the purchased railroad sections.

[2] John Adair was a well-to-do upper-class Irishman who settled in New York and married into the prominent Wadsworth family. Having become interested in the West on a buffalo hunt, he moved to Denver, Colorado. Some time later, he was introduced to Charles Goodnight, a frontiersman familiar with Texas, and the two established the J. A. Ranch.

By the time Adair died in 1885, the ranch comprised some 600,000 or more acres of land, 50,000 head of cattle, improvements that included the finest ranch headquarters in the Panhandle, 20 or 30 tanks, as many corrals, and innumerable widely scattered camps.

[3] The Diamond F outfit had its beginning in 1883 when, through the efforts of B. B. Groom, the Francklyn Land and Cattle Company was organized and 631,000 acres of land in Gray, Roberts, Hutchinson, Greer, and Carson counties were bought from the New York and Texas Land Company, which at the time controlled over 5 million acres of land acquired through the purchase of railroad scrip. The Diamond F holdings, bought with English and American capital, came later to be known as the White Deer Lands and as such played an important part in the settling of the country. Upon the establishment of the ranch, its promoter and his son Harry Groom became resident managers at respective salaries of ten and eight thousand dollars.

In doing this, he was acting in accord with an accepted custom. With the exception of the XIT Ranch, which was given to the Farwells in solid blocks in payment for erecting the Texas capitol, and the Diamond F, every other ranch in the Panhandle was following the same practice.

From the beginning, it was Bill's idea to put cows on the ranch proper, but steers on the free grass of the unprotected range outside. Since the Sacra and Sugg cattle were already on the ranch and were mostly cows, he included them in the ranch deal. They wore the Bar O brand. The purchase of a large herd of steers, to add to the three hundred that were among the Bar O cows, was planned for the immediate future. It would not have been possible to put together a trio of three partners more unpromising than Bill, Ralph, and William's father.

Bill, while still a boy, left Gettysburg College to try his hand at buffalo hunting in Kansas. From Kansas he moved to Colorado where he ran a freighting outfit[4] for his older brother's tannery. From Colorado he moved on to Texas. By chance, he made the acquaintance of Charles Goodnight, who offered him the contract to fence the J. A. Ranch. His only knowledge of cattle raising was picked up casually while living at the J. A. headquarters during the days of the fencing contract. Jefferson, the son of a high-ranking Washington official, was well educated (he both sang and spoke French fluently), handsome, and socially prominent. Unfortunately, he preferred such dilettante pastimes as acting in amateur theatricals to working. At the other extreme was William's father, who was sober, industrious, and intellectually inclined, the kind of man who succeeds by virtue of hard work and integrity.

Bill's first step after negotiating for the ranch was to take advantage of a new land law that enabled him to file on seven sections adjoining the ranch. This land was not only valuable, but of great beauty. It lay at the foot of the North Plains, directly below the cap rock escarpment in which arose the headwaters of the Salt Fork. Since the Salt

---

[4] Koogle may have been a partner in the tannery, a very successful operation that tanned buffalo hides. Regional Indians decorated the hides, many of which were exported to England.

Fork started out as a draw or dry-wash on the plains, it was not until it reached these headwater springs that it became a running stream. It was this stream that flowed directly across Bill's sections. The springs seeped through the rocks in various places, trickling down to form the lake that fed the creek. The lake was not large but deep and clear, and around the edge was a wide fringe of slough grass. To one side arose a clump of tall cottonwood trees. It was a beautiful location for a home, almost like an oasis in the desert. By claiming this area Bill added several thousand very valuable acres to the original ranch purchase.

When the time arrived for William's father to move to Texas, the thought occurred to Koogle that he might solve several problems by relinquishing his house in Clarendon to the newcomers and moving his own family and the ranch headquarters out to the newly acquired acreage. In the first place, the lake section occupied a central position between the ranch and the open range. Furthermore, in order to procure the land from the state as a settler, he was required to put a certain number of acres under cultivation, to build a habitation of sorts, and to spend a certain amount of time there. He would build a bunk house and kitchen for the boys and, for Carrie, a stone house more pretentious than Judge White's in town.

To the west beyond the lake section lay thousands of acres of "unlocated"—or unsurveyed—land with an abundance of grass but no living water. Between the springs that formed the headwaters of the Salt Fork and those which formed Dixon Creek in the Canadian River region, the only water came from rain-filled lakes. By possessing the Salt Fork, the ranch automatically came into control of about half of a free grass area that was twenty miles wide and forty miles long. Across the narrower portion of this expanse Koogle built a fence of the new and highly effective barbed wire. In order to escape paying to the state the rental demanded by the new lease law, he divided the fence into three five-mile sections with a mile and a half opening between each. These openings served for a time to appease the legislators who were already beginning to look with disfavor on the enclosing of unowned land. Since cattle are inclined to graze away from the wind, even a summer breeze, the purpose of the fence was to discourage the cattle of the new partnership from drifting too far northward in the summer and the northern herds from drifting southward in the winter. The enclosures were made solid, for all practical purposes, by "line riders"—cowboys whose one job was to ride the fence.

In 1885 the Panhandle was at the end of a long wet cycle. The creek waters ran deep; the marsh grasses grew tall; and even on the plains the lakes were numerous and the buffalo wallows well filled. It looked as if the new ranch would fulfill all of Koogle's promises.

By the time William and his family reached Clarendon, his uncle was already settled in the new house at the ranch, although his wife, Carrie, was still in Kansas City, awaiting the arrival of their second child. Five thousand steers had been taken to pasture by the ranch for Koogle and his wife's brother-in-law, Thomas Corrigan,[5] a prosperous Kansas City engineer. In handling cattle not belonging to the partnership, Koogle was attempting not only to add to his personal income but to the income of the ranch. No expenditure of ranch capital was required, and the work involved was negligible, since the steers would be turned loose on the free grass range each fall and gathered and shipped each summer along with the ranch steers. For this, the ranch would receive annually a stated sum per head. In the spring, shortly before the arrival of William and his family in Clarendon, Koogle made the down payment on three thousand steers and five hundred cows, which he had purchased for the ranch. Delivery would be made in August by the former owner, a South Texas stockman named Tandy. About the same time Koogle agreed to buy all the JB steers, cows, and bulls in Donley County. (At the time the cattle, owned by J. H. Brush, were being pastured on the Heart Ranch.) A brand, called the Half Circle K, in honor of Koogle, had been registered in the name of the three partners.

What William's father did not learn until after reaching Clarendon

[5] The firm was the firm of Corrigan, Lee and Halpin, which built the first Dallas Viaduct across the Trinity. William J. Smith and Corrigan consolidated the first horse and cable car lines that had been built in Kansas City in 1869 and 1886, built additional lines, and formed the Metropolitan Street Railway Company (information received from the Dallas Chamber of Commerce and the Kansas City Chamber of Commerce).

was that Koogle had assumed the $5,000 indebtedness still due on the Franklin school block, and that he had contracted for the JB cattle without having the money to pay for them. As a result, a few weeks after his arrival, William's father was persuaded to become a cosigner with Ralph and Koogle on a $25,000 note at 10 per cent interest to Brush.[6] The ranch was signed over as collateral.

CHAPTER IV

On reaching Clarendon, the stage stopped in front of a frame building, which Ralph, who was the town's postmaster, dignified by the name of post office. William jumped out to help unload. With the men laden down with suitcases, they went directly to the Jefferson house, where Cousin Em was waiting for them outside. Although the cottage, formerly occupied by Koogle's family, was ready for occupancy, the furniture from Maryland was not expected for two weeks. During the period of waiting, there was nothing William's parents could do but remain with Ralph and Em.

An extended visit with the Jeffersons was a plan that did not suit William at all. Besides not being overly fond of Ralph, he was uncomfortable with Em, a faded-looking, little woman who rarely spoke and lived in a house with religious pictures and a crucifix in every room. There was one compensation, however. With no chores to do, he would have ample time to explore his new home town and the immediate countryside around it—but not in knickers and a ruffled shirt. Early the following morning, he approached his father about getting more suitable clothes.

"You may be right," his father agreed. "There's an old saying which

[6] It is a question whether the loan was a personal, a bank, or a Brush interests loan. The three Brush brothers apparently controlled the Osage National Bank of Osage, Iowa; J. H. Brush was the president, J. P. Brush, the vice-president, and Avery Brush, the cashier. Judge White was their Panhandle representative. A letter from J. H. Brush to Judge White (1886) states, "Mr. Koogle has been here and I offered him a loan of $25,000.00 at ten percent for three years with option of two more. He offered me an interest in the ranch, but it seems to me he is paying a strong price."

suggests we do as the Romans do when in Rome. We'll walk down to the general store in a little while and see what we can find for you."

Although the store bore the name of B. H. White and Company, it was owned by the partnership of Morris Rosenfield and Judge White. Rosenfield, called "Rosie" by the townspeople, was in full charge. The store, usually called "Rosie's," delighted William. He could have happily spent the whole day looking. Apparently anything a buyer might wish for was there for sale. Bridles, saddles, guns —all kinds of cowboy gear—were on display, side by side with less exciting merchandise, such as washboards, tubs, and brooms.

When William finally made his selections, he found himself in a quandary. The pants were not difficult, since his mother had stipulated something less expensive than doeskins and more practical, but the shirts were a problem. They must be colored because he wanted to look like a regular cowboy; on the other hand, they must not be too loud. His father did not suggest a hat, and he did not mention one.

As he chose the last shirt, William heard the merchant[1] say to his father, "I know how much store a woman places on her possessions, so, when word comes that your shipment has arrived in Harrold, I'll forget about getting new merchandise for a few days, and I'll loan you Bill Ross, the best bullwhacker in the Panhandle. He'll put every piece down at your door in exactly the condition it left Maryland."

Seeing that William had finished, he said to him, "Maybe you would like to change clothes here. Would you, young man?"

William quickly accepted the offer. A few minutes later he came out from behind a pile of boxes, proudly wearing a yellow shirt and his first pair of blue jeans.

When he saw his sister, on reaching home, he laughed and said, "Katie, you had better find some need for going to the store. While Mr. Rosenfield was selling me my clothes, I noticed that he had two

---

[1] When William reached manhood, Rosie insisted that he buy a suit of evening clothes. By way of argument the merchant said, "You are a lot smater than any of these English dudes we have around here; you must show them that you can be as well dressed."

clerks. One of them was an old man, but the other one was a fine-looking young man just about your age."

Soon afterwards William learned that the older clerk was the Reverend Mr. Stanton, a retired Methodist minister, and that the younger man whom Rosie called Ben was Benjamin White Chamberlain, whose mother was a sister of Judge White.

William spent his entire first afternoon wandering around Clarendon. Certainly nothing he encountered bore any resemblance to the building in which he had lived in Maryland or to his father's store, which had occupied the first floor of the house. Many of the places of business, as well as the dwellings, were crude structures of adobe, with which he was not familiar. One was a square shack made of blocks of sod piled one atop another and a roof of apparently nothing more than many leafy branches. He could not figure what held the roof up. Maybe someday he would meet the owner and be able to go inside and find out. The more substantial buildings were of rock or lumber. All of them seemed to have been placed at random, without regard to size or use. One house was cut off from the others by a white picket fence.

When he came in to supper, still excited by all he had seen, he said to his father, "You should go with me tomorrow. This is a very funny place—a town without any streets on a river without any water."

His father laughed, and his laugh showed that he, too, had noticed the unusual character of their surroundings, particularly of the Salt Fork, which followed a subterranean course with no indication of its presence other than a small trickle of water in a wide expanse of sand.

The next day his mother suggested to William that he go with her to see their new home. It was a pleasant surprise to find that it was the cottage with the fence. It was larger than Em's, making it possible to have a parlor as well as two bedrooms, a dining room, and a kitchen. There were only two drawbacks—the well was some distance from the house, and the kitchen had to serve as the bathroom.

"You should like living here," his mother said as they closed the kitchen door and stepped into the backyard. "It's a good house. Bill freighted all the lumber in from Dodge City, and there is Eagle Hill not more than two hundred feet away."

"What is Eagle Hill?" William asked, seeing nothing but a small elevation with a flagpole on top.

"Why don't you go and see? Your uncle says it was built as a barricade against the Indians."

With a bound William was off. At the top he stopped to wave before running down.

"There's nothing there," he said as he rejoined his mother, "just the pole and a few piles of rock. What do you mean—Indian attack?"

"Well, until a few years ago this whole part of the country belonged to the Indians. When the ranchers and settlers began to move in, the Indians did as all people do to keep others from taking their land; they attacked the intruders and tried to destroy their settlements. But the government keeps them in reservations now, and they are not so dangerous. At least, that's what your uncle says. Anyway, the road over there on the right goes to Mobeetie and Fort Elliot. If the Indians come, the soldiers can get here right away so there's nothing to be afraid of."

"Really, Indians, Mother?" The thought even was exciting. "Just imagine. We live in Indian country."

The furniture reached Clarendon two weeks later, as expected. Rosenfield, having been notified of the outfit's departure from Harrold, was able to predict the time of arrival fairly accurately. William's father and mother and Ralph waited at the house, but William, in his eagerness, stationed himself at a vantage point on the bluff. He had already learned that watching the stage or a freight wagon cross the river was the most exciting event of the day. The fact that today's outfit was bringing the furniture from Maryland added to his interest.

When he heard the booming voice of Bill Ross cursing his oxen down the draw, he knew that the first wagon would soon be in sight. A few minutes later it was at the river's edge. All freight wagons were drawn by three teams: a "lead" team, a "swing" team, and a "wheel" team. Bill, as was usual, rode the wheel team animal to the right. From this position he was able to control the speed of his heavy, lumbering vehicle by a "jerk" rope that extended from his saddle horn, through the bridle of the righthand ox of both back teams, to a hand brake at the side of the wagon.

William watched with admiration. "What a smart man Bill must be to do such a difficult job. If I were only older, I could get Uncle Bill to teach me to be a bullwhacker." By then the wagons were getting close, and he turned to race back with the news to his waiting parents.

The unloading and uncrating got quickly under way. William worked eagerly with the men, taking things from the wagon to the house. Soon it was apparent that the small cottage would not accommodate all the furnishings of a two-story Maryland house.

Among the things that were giving the most concern was a rosewood spinet piano that had belonged to William's sister since early girlhood. Since Katie was musically inclined, her mother considered it not only one of the family's beautiful possessions, but a necessity as well. But, being practical, also, she realized that installing the instrument in the only logical place, the parlor, would destroy some of the room's usefulness as a sitting room. This must not be considered, since it was a long-established custom of the family to gather there in the evening to listen to William's father read aloud. After some discussion, however, it was decided that there was nothing that could be done but place the piano in the parlor—at least, until a more favorable location could be found.

The spinet was still in the packing box on the wagon. To lift it down and into the house promised to be a major job. Although the workers included not only the bullwhacker but several curious passersby, who had stopped to give assistance, it was William and a man none of the family had seen before that morning who were first up on the wagon. The man had attracted attention early, for although older and slighter than any of the others, he and the boy seemed to be doing most of the work. After pushing the box out of the wagon as far as possible with safety, they got down and began to pull. Just as it was most of the way out, the wagon gave a sudden lurch and catapulted the box to the ground. Both the man and William stumbled backward, escaping serious injury by a few inches. The instrument suffered no damage, but the stranger was enraged. For some reason he took the accident as a personal affront. With an amazing vocabulary, he damned God, the devil, and man, all in the same breath.

Then he turned to William's mother and shouted, "What's the matter with you? Why don't you put this God-damned son-of-a-bitch where it belongs? We'll never get it into the house, and, if we do, you'll never get it out. There's only one place in town, besides the old warehouse and the basement of the store, that's big enough to take it, and that's the saloon. If we had a good piano there instead of that old worn-out upright, we might have more people at Sunday's service."

After his tirade, he started walking irritably away in the direction of a pile of discarded packing boxes. As soon as he reached them, he began to rummage among them, as if in search of a plank or some object sturdy enough to be of help in moving the spinet.

Meanwhile, William had joined his startled parents to whom Rosie was saying, "I haven't met this man yet, but I feel certain he is the new Methodist preacher who has recently moved into the picket house across from Parks. He didn't mean any harm. We've had a steady stream of ministers since the colony was established. Like the rest, he'll stay a short while, then move on, and no one will ever know where he came from or where he went. In any case, I think his idea about the piano is not half bad."

But William's mother remained adamant. The piano must go into the parlor. By the time this difficult feat was accomplished, they had all become friends and had promised the minister, the Reverend W. A. Cooper, to attend services the next time he preached in Clarendon.

On the following Sunday the helpful stranger, much bescrubbed and subdued, held services for a congregation consisting of a handful of Methodists, a few cowboys, and the newly arrived Episcopalian family. Rosie, the Jew, who had a beautiful voice, was soloist for the day. On the way home to dinner with William's parents, the minister told them he had recently been assigned to the district by the Methodist Conference and would divide his time between Mobeetie and Clarendon.

After dinner, William accompanied Cooper and his wife back to the picket house in which they lived. As they reached the door, the minister said to William, "You seem to be a good boy; maybe you would like to do something for the church every now and then? Preacher Carhart came out here to convert the Panhandle to Methodism. He brought from Chicago that big old bell that hangs on the scaffold not too far from your house because it has a voice that can be heard for miles. I don't know how many folks are around that need converting, but going to church never hurt anyone. The son of one of my Methodist brethren is supposed to ring the bell, but he lives up the creek on a ranch and doesn't always get to town. So, if you don't hear that bell in time, I want you to run to the scaffold and pull that rope hard and long, so everyone will know a Christian service is about to begin."

William agreed eagerly. Swinging onto the bell rope would be fun, and he liked the idea of an important job, even one without pay. He did wish, however, that the offer had come from someone other than a preacher. Unfortunately, the opportunity for him to ring the bell never arose.

CHAPTER V

In a few weeks the cottage was in order, and life was becoming routine, even though it had required a complete change of habits for the whole family. William's mother and sister were busy getting used to managing a household without servants, and his father was busy acquiring, if possible, some knowledge of the cattle business, although he had no intention of taking an active part in the management of the ranch. He, like Jefferson, would be a silent partner; he would keep the books but would leave the cattle business to his brother-in-law, Bill, the only one the three partners who supposedly knew anything about stock raising. As for William, each day was filled either with chores at home or with new experiences of which there seemed to be no end. Since he was young and strong and a boy, he was expected to lighten the women's labors as much as possible. He was even called on to do the washing when contact could not be made with the wife of the stage and keeper at Bushey Creek.

His most onerous task, however, was milking the four cows, which, to his disgust, Koogle had been forced to bring into town to please William's mother, who refused to drink canned milk while living in cattle country. Not only William's lack of skill, but the nature of the animals added to his difficulties. They were not milk cows, but wild range cattle with baby calves. Since his uncle was insistent that the calves suckle first, several cows were necessary. William and his father threw together a makeshift corral by stringing in a circle the discarded wagons and oxen yokes from Koogle's old freighting outfit. On seeing it for the first time, the former bullwacker roared, "What the Hell are you getting ready for—an Indian attack?

Despite the work and the nuisance of having the unsightly corral within view, the arrangement proved satisfactory in every way. The cows and calves thrived on the lush creek grasses, and although there was not too much milk there was an abundance of butter, since the last of the milking is the richest. However, it was William who benefited most. At his uncle's suggestion, the cattle were turned loose each day to graze at a place some distance from the house. To facilitate the work of rounding them up and driving them back and forth, Bill sent a horse in from the ranch for William. It was only an old cow pony that had outlived its usefulness on the range, but it was William's chief pride. It compensated in a measure for the fact that he knew nothing about the ranch that was the reason for his being in Texas, and that, wish as hard as he might, his uncle never offered to take him back to headquarters for a visit. Early each morning and again at sundown, he and Tex jogged across the prairie like any cowboy and his mount. Although William had never ridden before coming to Texas, from the moment he mounted Tex he was completely at home in the saddle.

In his spare moments, he undertook the building of a lean-to. Since the cottage had only two bedrooms, William had to sleep in the parlor; when Uncle Bill came to town, the boy had to lay his pallet in the kitchen. Although Bill's visits to town were not frequent, his habit of appearing at the most unexpected times made the arrangement a nuisance since the kitchen did not make ideal sleeping quarters. Having discovered the piano box to be in good condition, he started to work. First he ripped off the sides. From these, he made a makeshift floor and exterior wall. With the rest of the lumber and additional pieces from other discarded crates, he made the framework for a slanting roof and one enclosed end. After attaching the roof to the house, he nailed tarpaulin over all the exterior except the opening for the entrance. During a hard rain, it would leak, he knew; and it would not offer much protection against winds and cold, if the coming winter proved to be as severe as everyone predicted. Also, it was only a cubbyhole with room for a sofa and a chair, but it was his own, and it gave him the freedom to go and come as he pleased. Even later, when his uncle's visits became fewer and farther apart, he was unwilling to move back into the house. To humor him, his parents did not insist.

During his first months in Clarendon, William had discovered that there were only four boys in that part of the Panhandle; only two could really be counted, for long, lanky Will Murdock, who was the son of the Quarter Circle Heart Ranch manager, lived several miles up the creek at the ranch headquarters. Furthermore, Will's father kept him so busy that he did not have time even to talk when another fellow stopped by. The family of William's Maryland cousin and chum, Bernie Rhoderick, had recently arrived in Clarendon but had settled on a farm too far away for the boys to see each other often. The only available companions left were the "little socks,"[1] who lived with their widowed father, Dr. Stocking, in the rooms behind the drugstore. William had never been inside the boys' living quarters, but he often wondered what a place would be like without a mother, and the thought made him sad.

---

[1] The Stocking boys spent part of their time with the Murdocks at ranch headquarters.

However, even though sympathetic toward the motherless boys, he had little time for them. It was not that he did not like them, but that the activities of boys no longer held his interest. The days were not long enough for him to see and do all the things he had in mind. He was very aware of the change taking place within himself. It was as if he had discarded some of his youth along with his knickers at Rosie's store. He wanted to be a part of the exciting life around him, of the men's world, and, as a result, he felt sure that his work, more often than not, was more fun than play would have been.

To his delight, he found there were many jobs a strong and willing boy could do. The men of the community liked him as well as he liked them, for he put himself out to be friendly, energetic, and responsible. Rarely a day passed without his running at least one errand for Rosie, and the nickels and dimes in the coffee can under his sofa came closer and closer to the top. Every morning after finishing his chores, he set forth on his routine rounds.

"Hi, Mr. Corbett," he called to the bootmaker as he passed his lean-to. And usually from within came the answer, "And a good morning to you, Billy. I am not too busy today. Why don't you step in and let me measure you for those boots?"

"Golly Moses, Mr. Corbett. You're in too big a hurry. Give me some time. The coffee can's not full yet."

It was a little private joke between them. From there, he hurried to the stage stand to see if there was hay to be stacked or thrown to the mules, and last of all, to Rosie's store. On the way home, he always stopped to talk to Bill Holden who was building bachelor quarters of sod for himself. If Bill's rheumatism happened to be giving him trouble that day, William lent him a hand in the stacking, working as steadily as if he were going to get paid. When he was late for dinner, his parents neither questioned nor chided him, and it made him feel proud and like a man to know they had confidence enough in him to let him come and go as he wished.

There were many hours during the long summer days, and he did not spend all of them in town. Often he saddled his horse and headed out the creek to idle away part of the morning or even the entire day.

These were the happiest times of all. There was never a lack of something to watch or to do. Every minute was filled with anticipation. The Carroll was a shallow but fast-moving stream. Three miles to the west was the Allen, in the sluggish waters of which were many holes. In those holes, bass, perch, and channel cat abounded. Between the two creeks was a wide stretch of level ground rising above the breaks on either side. Wild grapevines covered the walls of the cliffs, and on every ledge was a tiny plum thicket. All that was required for an outing was a sack of biscuit, a piece of bacon, and his uncle's old Winchester. He was glad he had learned to use a gun in Maryland.

It was difficult sometimes to maneuver his departure so as to escape the watchful eyes of the Stocking boys, who also had horses. But, if possible, he preferred to enjoy these outings alone. It was not that he was antisocial but that he had no need for the presence of another human being. As a companion, Tex sufficed. Tex went where directed and never had plans that interfered with those of his master.

The gully through which the Carroll coursed extended out in several places for a distance of perhaps fifty feet. On one such flat, a mile beyond town, lived the Tabors. A rock wall with a cedar log door marked the entrance to their dugout. In the space in front of it was the only orchard and garden in the Panhandle. It was irrigated by a bell-like contraption with a plunger that was kept in motion by the force of the creek. As it moved, water gushed out into a receptacle that overflowed into small irrigation ditches. The water-ram, as Tabor called it, held no interest for William, but he watched every stage of the garden's growth with delight, regretting only that he had discovered his friends too late to see the earth crack as the first green shoot pushed through. The old man was as pleased as William when an early flower turned to fruit.

"How many beans do you think we shall harvest from the first planting?" William asked.

Then, while they talked, Mrs. Tabor, sprightly and neat in her starched calico, appeared with cookies hot from the oven. After this, the visit was at an end, with William and his horse on their way to the next adventure. It was a good way to begin the day.

The prairies over which he roamed lay a thousand feet below the broad plateau that extended to the north and west. Although considered a part of the Great Plains, their protected position and abundance of water tempered the rigorous climate so characteristic of the true plains. They, too, were grasslands, the home of high winds, low rainfall, cyclones, hail, and blizzards, and their flora like that of the higher region had small leaves and large root systems as a defense against the droughts that were inevitable. But they were rolling ground swells instead of tablelands; the weather was milder, and the soil more fertile. Mesquite trees and shin oaks grew in profusion. Nesting in the plum thickets were prairie chicken, chaparral, and quail. In the cottonwoods along the creek were turkeys and an occasional hawk, and through the air flew catbirds, red-winged blackbirds, bluejays, doves, and the dirty and lazy cowbird, which fed off cattle parasites and left her eggs in an appropriated nest to be hatched by a more maternally inclined bird.

William watched the prairie birds with great interest. Having discovered the egg, he must investigate the nest and the bird that placed it there. As his knowledge and interest grew, there developed a kinship with his feathered friends. He enjoyed the sight of their bright bodies as they flashed across the sky, and their songs were not so much musical sounds as the chatter of a living presence he enjoyed.

Toward one prairie dweller, however, his attitude was not so kind. Having been warned by his uncle that the rattlesnake was the settlers' deadliest enemy, he moved with caution when afoot. Although a sluggish reptile that never attacked except when startled or trod upon, the rattler had the ability to coil and spring two-thirds its length with unbelievable skill. William learned to stop instantly at any sound that resembled the whirring of a katydid, to forego the pleasure of resting on a rock near the creek, and to look on the sunny ledges for the presence of a black-mottled, earth-colored body. In the manner of any true Westerner, he never failed to kill the enemy whenever he chanced upon him.

CHAPTER VI

In midsummer Judge White and his wife, Lottie, sent out invitations to an "open house." Except for the Parks's house, their home was the only one large enough to accommodate a number of people. William discovered quickly, on the evening of the party, that "open house" on the plains meant literally what the words implied. It was his and his family's first opportunity to see the people of the Panhandle as a whole. They were a heterogeneous assembly that ran the gamut of social and economic levels. At one extreme were Tabor and his mail-order wife whom he had procured through a matrimonial agency, and, at the other, the tall, gray-haired, and handsome but supercilious Britisher, the Honorable John Majoribanks Ashley, whose father was a baron and the chief stockholder in the Rockingchair Ranch. With him was a much younger brother, Percival, who on this occasion wore a frock coat.

In between were such men as Al Gentry, the first sheriff of Donley County, Stanhope and Bruce McClelland (Stanhope after graduating from Virginia Military Institute had come to Texas as an engineer for Gunter and Munson, first surveying job in the Panhandle—they had surveyed along the Canadian River), Alfred Rowe, owner of the R. O. Ranch, and Charles Goodnight, feudal lord of the Panhandle plains.

William would have recognized the Goodnights anywhere from the many descriptions he had been given of the Panhandle's most publicized couple. Mollie, who was famous for her bonnets and her interest in both the physical and spiritual welfare of her boys, arrived in a flowered lawn dress and a Stetson, around the crown of which was draped a long, pink veil. Goodnight, so big that he dwarfed every other man in the room by comparison, lumbered in like a buffalo. Everything about him had the same rugged and awe-inspiring quality as that of the plains. It was interesting to watch the faces of the other guests and to discover, from their expressions, their various personal reactions to the big man of the country.

The host, Judge White, was a tall, handsome, educated man. He had moved west in the hope of regaining his health, which had been impaired by long service in the Civil War. His wife, Lottie, was Carhart's sister.

The evening passed much too quickly for William. First, there were charades and music, with Ralph directing both; then, after refreshments—charlotte russe, cake, fruit punch, and coffee—had been served, the men and the women divided into two groups. Almost immediately, Vashti Parks, whose stately purple taffeta dress struck William as out of place in the West, started to relate to the women the latest Panhandle news.

"My husband tells me that a lot of gambling goes on in one certain room of the hotel. Do you see young Percival standing over there with your brother? Well, he lost five thousand dollars last week in what they said was a small, friendly game."

William, trying to listen in all directions at once, watched his mother closely at that particular bit of news. He knew she was well acquainted with her brother's weaknesses; and he could see her concern as she looked toward Bill and his young companion.

Among the men the conversation was taking a more serious note.

"The drought to the south," someone was saying, "may extend to include us, too, and the old-timers tell me that one season of extreme is always followed by another. The country is already overstocked. What will happen if the summer continues hot and dry as it has been so far, and a big freeze follows it next winter?"

"That would be a catastrophe," Judge White answered. "But why worry over possibilities when we should be giving our attention to more imminent matters? I hear on good authority that the Fort Worth and Denver, which started laying track again a few months ago, plans to rush construction so as to make certain the two divisions meet by the fall of next year; also, that the Southern Kansas will bisect the Panhandle from east to west. Railroads mean settlers, and settlers mean trouble for the cattleman. And that is not all. Leigh Dyer was in my office today. He still insists that he can save the railroad months of time and millions of dollars if he can persuade them to change their survey to approach the plains near Koogle's home section. Leigh should know, and he is positive that it is the only place where the ascent is gradual, where there is no river to cross, and no escarpment walls to dig through." Turning to Goodnight, he added, "What do you think about it?"

"Well, I've been to the place with Leigh, and he knows what he is talking about, all right; and the railroad engineer who is driving out with him tomorrow is inclined to agree. If so, the colony here will be by-passed by six miles."

At this point Parks interrupted to say, "I don't know much about the Fort Worth and Denver, but I do know about the Southern Kansas Railroad. It is almost ready to start laying track to the west. There is a colonization scheme for that part of the country. I am going to do the surveying so they can start locating their land. My crew is ready to leave town in a few days. I have a good engineer. All I need now is a second chainbearer. It's a job that doesn't require experience, and the work isn't too hard. The trouble is you can't get a man in this part of the world to do anything that isn't done on horseback."

William, who had been listening intently to all that was said, thought that here was a chance for him to do something exciting. He went over to Parks and said, "I should like that job very much ,sir, if you would let me have it."

The surveyor hesitated for a long second. "I don't know. You look a little young to me, and I certainly would hate to get to the middle of the Panhandle, and be forced to turn back so my chainbearer could get home to his mama."

There was something too patronizing and too facetious in Parks's tone for Rosenfield, who came to William's defense. "I guarantee that you'll find him more grown-up than a lot of your men. Furthermore, he's not only dependable, but I venture to say he has more energy than you have."

He was hired! In the next couple of minutes, he saw his mother's concern over her brother's gambling and the future of the colony transformed into concern over getting him—"You are barely fifteen, William!"—ready for his first job.

When he was about to leave the party with his family, Rosie said to him, "Drop by in the morning, and I'll help you get together the things you'll need for this kind of trip."

CHAPTER VII

As soon as his chores were finished on the following morning, William hurried to Rosie's.

"You are going on a surveying trip, not a cattle drive, I know. But you'll need many of the things that a cowboy has to have. Don't worry about paying me. You can do that after you get home."

As he talked, the merchant was pulling out a seven by sixteen-foot piece of ducking heavy enough to withstand the wind, sleet, and snow. Having gotten it off the shelves, he spread it on the floor and continued, "I'm no cowboy, but I've sold too many of these not to know what to do with them. Make your bed with the foot of the covers in the middle toward the wind. Your saddle must go at the head so that your water bag can be shoved under the saddle skirts for a pillow. If you don't have a saddle, use your clothes. You won't need a water bag this time either, but always remember to take one with you when you're alone on the plains. Besides, you must have a suggin, that's the cowboy name for comforter, and a blanket. I happen to have a good blanket, an army issue that old Roxy, Satterwhite's stagedriver, got off a soldier on a spree. And take good care of your bedroll because, after a horse, it's the most necessary part of a cowboy's equipment. You can't get a job without them." Then, as he finished wrapping the purchases, he added, "You should have boots, too. They are the best protection against snakes for a man on foot, but all good boots are handmade, and Corbett wouldn't have time to get them ready."

"Good," William thought, perfectly content. "They hurt my feet when I am on horseback. They would kill me if I were on foot, and this is a walking job." He had worn his uncle's boots once, and he knew.

He was grateful for Rosie's interest and flattered by his willingness to let him buy on credit, but the idea of being in debt bothered him. There might be another way. As soon as he reached home, he got out the coffee can that served him as a safe and dumped its contents on the floor. After counting the pile of nickels and dimes and quarters, he found to his delight that he had enough to pay for everything he had bought. He could leave home without a thing on his mind except being the best chainbearer Parks had ever had.

Long before the other members of the party were gathered, William, with his bedroll, stood waiting in front of the B. H. White and Company door. The usual surveying outfit consisted merely of a buckboard, a chuck wagon, a "hoodlum," and horses for a crew of seven. The cook drove the chuck wagon, a huge tarpaulin-covered vehicle in which the food, the cooking utensils, and the bedrolls of the crew were carried. It was the duty of the "hoodlum" driver to transport the surveying instruments and the chains, to water and stake the horses, to gather wood, if possible, and, if not, cowchips for cooking, and to help the cook.

Parks was very close with his money. As a result, the outfit was as meager as possible. There were five men in all. Parks and two of the men rode in a two-seated hack. William rode in the supply wagon, which was driven by the cook. In the wagon were not only the chains and necessary surveying equipment, but also the cook's potatoes, bacon, beans, flour, coffee, and Dutch oven. The oven was a shallow, iron pot on legs with a heavily rimmed top that held the coal necessary for the baking of biscuits.

There was no wood available on the plains, and since Parks had not gone to the trouble of adding wood to his supplies, buffalo chips were used as fuel. The first time William saw the cook place the bacon directly on top of the chips to cook instead of in the frying pan, he demurred. On seeing his questioning face, the cook grinned broadly and said, "Don't bother, son; them chips add a flavor to the bacon that you'll like as soon as you get used to it."

The cook had been a catcher of mustangs in his younger days. He dressed much after the manner of Daniel Boone, with pistols in his belt and Bowie knives stuck in his boots. It required only a few hours for William to discover that he was not nearly the ferocious fellow he wished to appear to be, but, in reality, was the mildest of men. He had been born in a stockade in Kansas. Upon the death of his mother, while he was still a baby, he had been tended by a squaw whose purpose was to rear the child according to the traditions of her tribe. By early manhood he was thoroughly schooled in the language and life of the Utes. He moved along from scout to soldier to buffalo hunter at Hidetown. Like the squaw foster-mother, the cook was intent on passing on to his fair-skinned companion all the things he had learned in his long and varied life. Like many other plainsmen, he was unable to converse readily with another, but, if uninterrupted and permitted to think aloud, he could talk for hours of the life he had led and the things he thought every boy should know. In later years, long after William, too, had become a plainsman, he often remembered the first thing the old man ever said to him. They were crossing the narrow flat between the Carroll and the Allen, and as they passed a mesquite, the cook pointed toward it and said, "We're goin' to have a hard winter, son. Look how full and long them bean pods are. That's nature gettin' ready to protect the cattle. We are due for a drought, and after a drought comes the freeze. When the grass is gone, the mesquites will feed the cattle."

The crew's route followed the stage road to Tascosa, out from town along the creek, past the Heart headquarters, on to the Allen, and around the mound called Bull-cob Mountain, and up on to the plains. Except for a ride or two along the border, William had never really seen the plains before. Once out upon them, he found himself on a limitless, trackless expanse of tableland. The only water came from the salt licks or buffalo wallows. The grass was much shorter than it had been around Clarendon. Not a bird was to be seen. Other than the outfit, there was no visible life anywhere; no sound to be heard, nothing to see but land, land, land; miles of it on every side. About nine each morning a hot, dry wind arose to blow ceaselessly till sundown. In a country so barren of features, the heavens were man's only ever-present, everlasting guide.

"Remember," the cook said, "the sun always rises in the east and sets in the west, and the North Star always points north. But it aint able to point that way without the help of two other stars and the Big Dipper, so you must know about them, too. They git tired o' one place and change around through the year, and you got to remember where they will be next month as well as this."

As they drove past the first water hole, the cook continued, "That's a buffalo wallow. I guess it got started years ago when the first herd stopped to lick the salty earth, and, as they kept on a'comin' year after year, they tramped the earth down so hard the water couldn't git out, and the first thing anybody knowed, there was a little pool.

"Now, look at everyone of 'em good as you pass, and you'll see that no two's alike. Each one has a size and shape all its own, and that very little difference between 'em may help you find your way home, sometime."

Because the wagons were all heavily loaded, their progress was slow. It was well up into the afternoon of the second day before they reached the location where work was to start. It was some sixty miles from Clarendon. Parks was an early riser and hard master, and within a short time a routine had been established.

In ordinary field notes, all that was required was to define the limits of a tract by making marks denoting such natural objects as trees, hills, rivers, or gullies, and the distance between them. In an empty expanse, such as the plains, it was necessary, instead, to relate all the lines to true meridians and parallels ascertained through various heavenly bodies. The next step after establishing the meridian was to sink the initial stake and pin, then start measuring with a chain in a direct line toward the flag-bearer. Parks, like other surveyors of his day, was using a Spanish unit of measurement—something less than three feet and called a vara. The chain, which was fifty varas long, was so heavy that it required two men to handle it. The back chain man held it secure to the pin while the lead man pulled it in a line with the flag. When the chain was stretched full length, another pin was put down, after which the rear man pulled up the discarded pin and moved ahead with the chain to repeat the procedure. Ten or twelve miles a day could be surveyed. At each section corner, four trenches were dug around a small square on which the loosened sod was later piled to form an elevation. On top of this was placed a marker, with even numbers marking the school sections and odd numbers those of the railroad. Since the markers were always pointed in one direction, they served the settlers both as a guide and a compass. This was the kind of work William had agreed to do.

By sunup Parks had his instruments set up and was busy with them.

From then until sundown, stopping only to eat, William and the men pulled pins, dragged the chain, and dug sod. The heat was stifling and rose upward in steady waves that formed a mirage of lakes on the distant horizon, as if to mock the sweating and thirsty laborers. Often it was necessary to dig down into the basin of a dried lake to find water for man and beast.

One morning as William dragged his chain, he saw moving toward him at the side an unusually large snake. Unlike the ordinary rattler, this one appeared to have no intention of fleeing from the enemy, but was coiling for the strike. It was about eight feet long, which meant it had a thrust of over five feet. There were no rocks around, and William had no gun. To hit at it with the chain would have required too close proximity for safety. He jumped away, shouting for help as he went. One of the men came running. As he approached, the coiled snake raised its fierce head and rattled ominously. It was preparing to strike when one shot from the man's pistol put an end to its life.

The days became weeks, and the weeks became a month. By the end of August the crew had surveyed in a northwesterly direction for a distance of seventy miles back and forth. Only a few more days of work lay ahead of them. One night William had an unusually interesting experience. It had become his habit to pitch his bedroll near the place where the horses were staked to graze through the night. That particular day had been long and difficult, for Parks was pushing the men to finish the survey. William had been asleep only a few minutes when he was awakened by a restless movement among the animals nearest him. Sitting up, he saw moving toward them a stallion of great beauty. Warily, almost like a dancer, the stallion put one foot down and then another, as if on guard in the presence of enemies. It was bright moonlight, and, in the distance, William discerned what appeared to be a small bunch of horses. They were certainly following their leader, but at a safe distance behind him. Slowly the stallion moved to within a few feet of the mares, stopped, then turned to make a circuitous run back to the others. Once there, he raised his head in a defiant gesture, snorted, and, with tail flying, raced into the shadows, his companions following in hot pursuit. The thundering of their hooves awakened the men.

"That's just an old mustang stallion, trying to get our mares to follow him," the cook said. "They always run in bunches with a leader like the horse you saw. When I began hunting on the plains, they all had a wide black stripe down their backs and sometimes on their legs, but they've mixed up so much with army horses that they don't look too different no more."

Within a week of the episode, the work was finished, and the outfit turned back toward home, following the stage road most of the way in. The part of the country that they recrossed on the first day lay to the south of the Canadian River. There were more creeks, and the lakes were more numerous than in other areas of the plains. Even though absorbed in the cook's tales, William scanned the landscape continually as he listened. He felt not only acutely aware of everything around him but also in complete harmony with it. His every sense seemed attuned to catch each sound, each smell, and each slight change of scene.

Their slow progress in the chuck wagon over the vast expanse of monotonous plains made even the most trivial incident seem significant. One midafternoon, his attention was attracted by an unusual pair of animals in the distance. He remembered the place from the journey west because the outfit had camped there one night. The grazing animals were not mustangs, according to the cook, for there were only two of them. They were not antelope, or they would have fled at the sound of the approaching wheels. Besides, antelope, like mustangs, moved in bunches. Neither did they resemble cattle. As they drew close enough to recognize them, both William and the cook were amazed to discover that the animals were mules; evidently a strayed work team. They paid no attention as the wagon rattled by.

"Belonged to some settler," the cook mused, "but they're shore a long way from home."

They reached Clarendon the following afternoon. Proud and happy, William took his place at the end of the line to receive his pay. When his turn came, Parks extended a hand in which there was no money, patted him on the head as if he were a child, and said, "You, my boy, have received the best wages of anyone in the crew—

experience, and experience that will be worth much more than dollars and cents to you in future years."

For a moment, William was too astonished to realize what had happened. Surely his employer was joking. It was true that he was just a boy, but a boy who had done a man's work, and he deserved to be paid like everyone else. By the time Parks walked away, William knew that he must accept the inevitable. An ugly trick had been played on him, but no one must see that he was humiliated. With tightly pressed lips, and without a word to the men with whom he had worked so happily for five weeks, he turned and started home. As he trudged along, he made a solemn vow to himself that this would never happen to him again. He was certain he had learned a lesson he would never forget.

CHAPTER VIII

The first thing William noticed on his return was the great change that had taken place in the colony during his absence. For the second time in its existence, the building designed by Carhart for a combination school and church had been made into a saloon with gambling tables. Aunt Carrie and her two children had returned from Kansas City and were established in their new house at the ranch. Bill, however, was seldom with them.[1] He rarely visited with his sister in town, and William noticed that his uncle's behavior seemed to be a matter of great concern to both his parents. Leigh Dyer's contention that there was a more accessible route to the plains than the one originally indicated had been substantiated by the railroad officials, and a new survey was under way.

Already William's father had reached the unhappy conclusion that his residence in Texas was not to be as short as he had anticipated. Also, if the town was to be moved, as Judge White had suggested at the open house, a home for William's mother would have

---

[1] Letter from J. H. Brush to Judge White. "Mr. Koogle does not seem to have received any of my letters as dispatched. He has not remained in any one place long enough."

to be built. Because of the lack of servants and the difference between their past and present way of life, the new house would be planned on a much smaller scale than that of their Maryland home, even if slightly larger than Koogle's cottage. In such a case, there would be no further advantage in leaving stored in Rosie's basement either the small remnant stock brought from Maryland or the furniture for which there was no longer any use. Both might bring a good price if put up for sale in Clarendon where all articles of merchandise were scarce. It was an added inducement for William's father, who had never before been idle, to get back into business.

Unfortunately, the only available space suited to the kind of small shop he had in mind was in the post office. He was certain that Ralph would be more than agreeable to the idea. Although there was little work involved in sorting two bags of mail a day, Ralph's constant presence as the federal agent in charge was necessary. To assist in passing his many idle hours, he had installed a few shelves on which to place small groceries. Ralph would be the grocer, and William's father the dry goods merchant.

An agreement between the two was quickly reached. The grocery shelves would remain as they were, but the post office equipment would be moved to the back. Since it consisted mainly of a few lettered cigar boxes for certain people's mail and a sack on the floor for the remainder, it required little space and left ample room for the tables and shelves needed by William's father. There was, however, no room for any but small articles of merchandise.

The post office, which was on the main road through town, was well located for business. Parks's office was on the same side, and the courthouse and B. H. White and Company were directly opposite. The piece goods were piled on tables inside, but the furniture was lined up, a few pieces at the time, on the boardwalk outside, within view of all who happened to pass. On the opening day, fourteen rocking chairs were sold to an equal number of delighted housewives.

It was while the sale was in progress that the surveying crew returned home. For the first few days, William was busily occupied assisting in the heavy work of uncrating furniture and transporting it from warehouse to store. His bitter disappointment at failing to receive the wages due him was tempered by the air of excitement that pervaded the atmosphere, with the furniture sale and the newly opened saloon the two focal points of interest. William passed the saloon many times each day as he plied back and forth between home, warehouse, and post office. That it was operated by two strangers, he felt certain. The same two men were always visible through the window, and he had never seen either before. He had noticed one of them in particular because he was young. One morning this particular partner happened to be outside tacking something onto the wall by the door as William passed.

On seeing William, he turned and called out, "Wait a minute. Aren't you the Lewis boy? Well, I'm Bill Menasco. My partner and I just moved in."

When William answered in the affirmative, the man continued, "We need someone to clean up and run errands for us. Would you like the job?"

William thanked him but refused with the excuse that he helped his father and had no time for anything else. He would have liked very much to work for someone outside the family, and his curiosity about the activities within a gambling hall and saloon gave the offer special appeal. Being aware, however, of the stern reaction such a suggestion would arouse in his parents, he was careful not to mention the encounter.

While the saloonkeeper was talking, William's eye was caught by the large lettering on a newly displayed poster, tacked on the outside wall. "Fifty dollars' reward for the return of a pair of fine work mules," it read.

On seeing William's interest, the man explained, "Old Gatherin lost some mules out on the plains a while back. He's the fellow that handles the work teams for the railroad's construction crews. He's such an old drunk that I wonder he ever missed 'em."

"Mules on the plains! That's what we saw."

As William continued on his way, his mind was on nothing else, but he mentioned the incident to no one and worked as usual until the store was closed.

By the time he sat down to supper, his decision was made. He remembered exactly where he had seen the animals and knew the place was not more than fifty miles away. He could make the trip in four days. If the team had not strayed too far, he felt confident he would be able to find them and get them back to town alone. If he could, the reward money would more than compensate for not getting the wages due him as chainbearer.

His mother demurred in the beginning but was finally persuaded to accept his plan. Although his father said nothing, William sensed that he did not understand why anyone would be so eager to go off alone in a strange country—and with so much confidence and so little fear.

William was up and off the next morning long before dawn, equipped with his bedroll, his water bag, a sack of biscuit and bacon, and his Uncle Bill's Winchester. His chief concern was to get out of town without being seen by the Stocking boys, and to get beyond the Heart headquarters before Will Murdock, who was always outside the ranch house, could see him pass by. It was not his intention to share the reward. The trip had to be made alone.

He followed the stage road as Parks's crew had done, up the creek and out upon the plains. The region where the Allen ran into the Carroll was brushy and heavily wooded, a favorite roosting place for turkeys. The idea come to him that a young bird roasted over a campfire would be a welcome change from bacon and biscuit. He stopped, dismounted, tied his horse, then crept slowly to the top of the flat. There were no turkeys in sight, but to his amazement, he saw, in the distance on the other side, what appeared to him in his fright to be a large Indian encampment. There were several squaws, numerous children, and a few braves. Had he been as familiar with the country as he later came to be, he would have known that it was only a runaway band from the reservation, out to hunt and steal for a few days. But he knew none of this, and he had never before seen an Indian. Terrified, he mounted his horse and galloped off. After a while, his alarm subsided, and, finding himself at a safe distance away, he stopped to rest Tex.

Even the presence of a supposed enemy failed to act as a deterrent to his plan. Within the hour he was well on his way again. For the remainder of the day he jogged along at a slow pace, mindful that both he and his horse had to take it easy on a long trip. He stopped only to eat and to water the horse. He saw many bunches of antelope, but they were out of gunshot range, and about noon he passed the down-stage from Tascosa.

Roxy pulled his teams in long enough to call out, "What's a kid like you doin' way out here by yourself? Ain't you afraid you'll git lost?" William grinned and shook his head.

By dusk he was far from home and civilization of any kind. Tascosa was eighty miles from Clarendon. The only habitations in between were the ranch headquarters and the stagekeeper's dugout. One was far behind and the other far ahead. It had been many hours since he left town, and both he and his mount were in desperate need of food and rest. Since the lakes he sought were still some distance away, he decided to make camp where he was, in the middle of the bald prairie. In the absence of trees or some other natural hitching post, his first chore after watering and unsaddling his horse was to dig a narrow trench in which to bury and tramp down the knotted end of the long rope that was tied to Tex. It was a tedious job to dig into the hard, dry ground with only a knife for a tool. Having accomplished it, he gathered sufficient cow chips to last the night and started a fire. After eating, he spread his bed at a comfortable distance between its protective light and the grazing horse, and settled down for the night.

Sleep did not come quickly. An intense feeling of loneliness arose within him, as if this were all the world and he was the only human in it. As far as he could see, the plains stretched out endlessly, to disappear beyond the dark horizon. Everywhere there was deadly silence. Once a bullbat with his shrill, strong whistle shot through the air, almost close enough to be touched. Occasionally the barking laugh of a coyote came from far away, or a cicada whirred. Otherwise, there were only the tiny crackling sounds that came from the dungheaps as the worms worked through them, or the stir of the grass as his horse moved from place to place. For hours, he lay with his eyes on the heavens, and, as he looked, he remembered the fanciful stories his father used to tell him about the stars. As his glance came to rest on the North Star, he wondered how one object could mean so many things to different people: a fairy tale to his parent, but a priceless clock and compass to the buffalo hunter. Above him the tail of the Big Dipper was pointing downward.

"It is midnight," he thought and closed his eyes in slumber.

He slept past daylight, awaking to find threatening clouds scattered over the sky. There was still a distance of possibly fifteen miles to cover before he would have to turn off the stage road. He could not miss it, since it was the place where Kilfoil always deposited his collection of buffalo bones while on a bone-hunting trip. The haul to town was made at the completion of his search. When William reached the spot later in the morning, curiosity forced him to alight. Before him, rising like a monument, was a huge pile of bones gathered from a radius of many miles. As he looked, he wondered if Kilfoil made money at so unusual an occupation, and, if so, whether it might not be a good thing for him to take up until the age to become a cowboy arrived. A crude circle of green was painted around the pile with a K on one of the larger bones. This was the only proof of ownership. In spite of this, according to William's father, no trespasser ever disturbed the collection, although everyone knew it would bring a good price on delivery to the button factory.

The three lakes, which were his destination, were off to the right of the road. Although the sky was completely overcast, he felt certain the rains would not come soon and that, since the lakes were easily seen from a distance, he could find them without difficulty. He reached the first one after a short ride. There were no mules in sight, but far away at the back of the farthest lake he noticed what appeared to be a bunch of mustangs. Although he galloped the first part of the way, he slowed down on drawing near them, for mustangs were keen of sight and hearing. At the warning sound of hoofbeats, the sentinels returned to the main body of animals, watching him all the while. He was barely near enough to distinguish one from the other when the bunch turned to run with all speed from the lake.

Knowing that it was their habit to circle, then to return to the home range, he followed them. On and on they went tossing their proud necks as they ran.

After a while he noted that two of the animals were gradually dropping behind. It must be the mules, William thought, for no domesticated animal could possibly keep pace with those wild creatures of the plains. On and on they all raced, horse, mules, and mustangs, with the mustangs drawing ahead of the slower animals, but the horse gaining steadily on the mules. By the time the mules were overtaken, the mustangs were long out of sight.

Having tied the team to his saddle horn with ropes brought for the purpose, William remounted to start the ride homeward. As he did, he suddenly realized that he had no idea where he was. Much ground had been covered during the wild ride, and the lakes that were many miles away were his only landmark. The sky had grown dark and ominous, and rain was beginning to fall. Once again, as on the night before, a great feeling of being alone in the world engulfed him. He must get back either to the lakes or the road, but how? There were four directions in which to travel. Which of the four should he take?

At this point, as if in answer to his unspoken cry for help, he remembered what an old buffalo hunter had told him, "Don't move about when you're lost. Stay put wherever you are until you have a sure sign to guide you."

The only sure sign, he was afraid, would have to come from the sky, which was obscured by clouds and rain. He would follow the old man's advice, and make camp where he was for the night. Certainly no harm could come to him, and it never rained for long in the Panhandle. He had no way of telling how close it was to bedtime, but that made little difference. His sleepless night and the long day had wearied him, and he was more than ready to crawl under his tarp. After finishing his supper, however, he decided to make one last effort to find his way before the descent of complete darkness. With the staked mules as his center point, he began riding a wide circle around them, taking care to keep them always in sight. He was about halfway around when he saw a dark object rising ahead of him. As he drew nearer, it took on a familiar aspect. It was, as he suspected, a section marker, one of the many he had helped to put up. He still had only a vague idea as to his whereabouts, but of one thing he was certain: the stage road lay directly to the west. Using the marker as his compass, he easily figured the direction to take in the morning. Happily he rode back, staked his horse, replenished his fire, and spread his bed between Tex and the mules. Pulling the tarp up over the saddle horn to keep out the rain and feeling pleased with himself, he went to sleep.

He awoke at dawn, rested and eager, to be greeted by a bright, clean, and shining world. He was in Clarendon by midafternoon of the following day.

He put the team in the corral, then hastened to the saloon without stopping at home first to speak to his mother. The young saloonkeeper greeted him with a grin and inquired, "Where have you been? I haven't seen you pass here for several days."

He explained, ending with the "sir" he always used for older men.

"I told you my name the other day; I'm Bill Menasco, and if you and I are to be friends, don't call me 'sir.' Call me by my name. You are in luck today. The man you are looking for is over there at the card table. He was passing through and stopped in town for a day's relaxation."

William walked eagerly toward him, already imagining the pleasure Gatherin would evince on learning of the recovery of his team. Instead, the man did not even look up until after William had finished speaking, and when he did, he responded in a surly voice. "You know and I know that a kid like you wouldn't be able to go out onto the plains and bring back a pair of mules. I'll bet you stole 'em in the first place and have had 'em hidden out, just waitin' for me to get back to town."

Could it be possible, William wondered, that once again he was going to be done in by an unscrupulous man? Patiently, he gave details of the survey trip and of having seen the mules, and, also, of having passed Roxy as he went after them.

But Gatherin continued to argue. Suddenly Menasco came over to the table and, with a strong hand on the other man's shoulder, said, "You dirty son-of-a-bitch of a Scotchman. Shell out the money.

You know that youngster's telling the truth, and you'll either pay or never get another drink or gamble away another dollar in my place of business."

Gatherin meekly paid.

CHAPTER IX

During the following days, William was in a quandary. The fifty dollars not only constituted a considerable sum but had been earned by work that had been long and hard. It must be used to the best advantage. He had no doubts as to his ultimate goal, only about the best method of achieving it. He had felt from the beginning that he would never leave the West, and that, if he worked hard enough, someday he would have cattle of his own, grazing on the beautiful, rolling plains amid which he was living. But to become a cattleman, he must first be a cowboy, and to be a cowboy, he must have the proper equipment. He checked in his mind the things that Rosie had suggested as necessary on the day he was being outfitted for the survey trip. Tex, it was true, was old, and his saddle had seen hard usage before William got it from his uncle, but Tex and the saddle would do. Besides, a new horse and saddle were beyond his present means. As he had a good bedroll, the next things on the list were boots, spurs, and a pistol. Boots hurt his feet; he had tried them on and knew. He was not going to wear them if he could possibly get along without them. He could not imagine using spurs on a horse; so all that was left was the gun. There was one he had long admired at the store. On the other hand, there were some cows that Parson Allen had for sale. Allen had come to the colony originally to open a school. In the absence of pupils and a church, he had turned to stock raising. He lived near the Heart headquarters and made his living by keeping small herds of cattle long enough to fatten them for sale in lots of two or three to neighboring buyers. The choice lay between the cattle and the gun. He would go for another look at the pistol, and to ask Rosie's advice.

As William crossed the street, he was joined by Will Murdock, who remarked that he had been busy all week. The Heart Ranch had recently received a big herd from South Texas, and he had been helping put one hundred of the cows into Parson Allen's pasture. The trail drive up from South Texas had been hard, and some of the cows had not stood it too well. Ordinarily, William would have been eager to hear all Will had to say, but, on that particular day, he had his mind on other matters.

As they drew near the B. H. White and Company store, they saw several men trying to crowd through the door. They thought little of it for the store and the saloon were the two chief gathering places when an outfit came into town. The store itself was in a fifty-foot–deep building that had served originally as a storehouse for Carhart. Underneath was a basement in which could be found the most unusual of items. Although freighters, at regular intervals, brought in new merchandise, the original stock had been acquired at a bankruptcy sale of one of Sanger Brothers' subsidiary stores. As a result, it included articles not to be found in the usual dry goods establishment.

Furthermore, it was the depository for arms. Since the carrying of firearms was not permitted in the colony, some provision had to be made for the guns that all visitors wore into town. As a result, a long counter at the back of the store was reserved for one purpose only—to hold rifles and six-shooters. On occasion the pile grew high enough to suggest a miniature armory.

The store also served as the bank. There was practically no money in circulation, so checks became the usual legal tender. The nearest bank was at Harrold, which meant that all checks and money were placed for safekeeping in Rosie's basement vault. As a result, the store was the place to which everyone came sooner or later.

As William and Will Murdock crowded in with the others, loud voices could be heard from inside.

"Rosie has decided to raffle off the gun we have all been wanting but didn't have the money to buy," one of the bystanders explained to somebody.

The pistol in question was the one William was so interested in, a beautiful nickel-plated Colt forty-five, with a mother-of-pearl grip, and a hammer and barrel engraved with a dragon's and a dog's head. The two men who seemed to be the center of attention were strangers to William, but Will recognized one of them. He was a man named Wakefield who had made the first attempt to run a saloon in Clarendon. Through provisions of settlement in the colony, however, he was quickly forced to abandon it. Will Murdock's father was judge at the time, and for months afterward it was feared that the disgruntled saloonkeeper, who was known for his lack of scruples and a quick temper that had already resulted in one murder, might return to kill both Carhart and his legal advisor. This was the first time he had been in town since the unpleasant incident.

His companion was a much younger man, a rascally looking fellow, who most probably had never been on a horse. He wore a rattlesnake belt and the gunman's low-slung holster attached to his leg. It seems that earlier in the day, after a lengthy period of drinking, the two had gone to the store to make an attempt, by fair means or foul, to get the pistol. As their noisy argument over the price grew in intensity, a crowd of passersby began to gather. When the language of the two men reached the abusive stage, an onlooker suggested that Rosie not sell the gun but sell chances on it at five dollars each, a suggestion to which Rosie readily agreed, as he was eager to get the two troublemakers out of his store. Furthermore his profit would be larger.

The decision had just been made when a new argument arose, this time between the offenders themselves. One insisted that the lucky person be determined by a cut of the cards, the other by a throw of the dice. After listening to them for a while, Rosenfield, in exasperation, exclaimed, "This is my store, and I'll not have such goings-on in it. Here's the money for your chances. Take it and get out."

Because of the feeling of the crowd, the pair decided to accept the money and leave. When the draw was made later, the winner was Rosie himself. One of the tickets he had taken back had won. Embarrassed over the turn of affairs, he said, "I don't want the gun. Anyone who will give me ten dollars for my two chances may have it." But the crowd demurred. That was not fair since everyone had already paid for a chance.

"All right," Rosie agreed, "everybody shall have another chance and it won't cost too much. Instead of drawing a ticket, everyone will have to pitch a dollar at a marker on that far crack in the floor. I'll even give the two boys that weren't here before a chance to participate." And he added laughingly, "I'll also give them the dollars to pitch with, because in the end I'll get all the dollars anyway."

The boys pitched last and, as was to be expected, did not get even close to the crack. Someone they had never seen before won the pistol. William was disappointed but consoled himself with the thought that he had not really expected to get anything by merely pitching dollars at a crack. Even before this afternoon he had begun to wonder if cowboys ever wore such a fancy gun as Rosie's.

Within a week William had bought the cattle from Parson Allen: three fine, fat cows, one of them already with calf. Until he could find a more permanent home for them, he put them in the corral with the milk cows.

CHAPTER X

Shortly afterward, in early October, the Tandy herd reached town. On the following morning William and his family went to the ranch to watch Koogle receive and brand the Tandy cattle and to visit with Carrie for a few days.

Although the family had started from home soon after daybreak, the branding was well under way by the time they arrived at the ranch. As they drew near, William saw before him a scene unlike anything he had imagined. In the distance, several cowboys were holding the main herd, about three thousand steers; closer in was a smaller herd of cows and calves. Not far away the *remuda*—the relay of cow ponies—was held in readiness for the frequent change of mounts required by such grueling work. The boy in charge was a little Negro named Birl who was possibly thirteen years and whom none of the family had ever seen before. Branding irons were piled high, and near them was the bed of banked-down coals used to heat them, not red hot but to the proper temperature to sear the flesh. Two hands were busy digging up and dragging in from the creek the mesquite roots that served as fuel. Standing by was the roundup tally man, whose job it was to keep count of each animal branded.

The cutting horses appeared to be as accomplished as their riders. Once an animal was cut out and released to the men at the fire, the pony, apparently without direction from his rider, slowly returned to the herd, quickening his pace only when close enough to dart in after the next animal toward which he was pointed. When the running cow turned to the right to dodge its pursuers, the roper, leaning far to the same side, twirled his rope till the exact moment when his throw would make the proper catch. After this the cow was dragged across the prairie to the fire, where two cowboys on foot stood in readiness to secure the animal's legs and hold it down while the brander pressed his scorching iron against its hide. An additional mark, adopted by the Half Circle K to attest the ranch's ownership, was made with a knife on its ear. If it were a bull calf intended for the steer herd, the castrating was done at the same time.

It was not a pretty spectacle. On all sides could be heard the bellowing of a milling herd. Blood-bespattered men, flourishing branding irons and knives, cursed with fervid language the lowly creatures upon whom they were expending their labors. The mingled odor of sweat, smoke, fire, and burning flesh filled the air with a nauseating stench. The appearance of the cattle themselves added to the barbarity of the scene. Although decades of living under the harsh sun and wind of Texas and continuous crossbreeding with domestic cattle had greatly modified the appearance of the longhorn, he still gave evidence of his origin. He stood high off the ground on long, thin legs with narrow hips and sometimes with swayed back. He had wild eyes, big ears, and horns that were powerful although no longer curled.

Unfortunately, the Pecos herd was not only of inferior quality but was suffering the effects of both a drought and lack of care on the long drive from South Texas. There was no excuse for their not having trailed well, for they possessed qualities suited to the harsh and untamed land upon which they had developed. Like the men of the plains, the longhorn had great physical strength, endurance, and self-reliance. They had the ability to walk long distances, to climb, to swim, and to forage for themselves. The Sugg cattle, which had come with the purchase of the ranch, were also longhorns, but with an added strain of Durham. This strain and the effects of having grazed the long, nutritious grasses around the Carroll had greatly tempered their harsh appearance. The difference between the quality of the two herds was alarming. Later, William's father admitted to William that he had never before beheld anything so unpromising as the new cattle, and that he was disturbed.

The branding and the placement of the various herds required some time, so William remained at the ranch to take his turn with the little Negro at herding the horses and digging mesquite roots. It was an experience that filled him with deep satisfaction. It was the beginning of an involvement of body and soul in a kind of life which, although foreign to anything he had previously known, was just what he wanted. He was destined—although he did not yet know it—to be one of the fortunate few who are always at their best because they are doing that which they like most and which is most compatible with both their temperament and their talents. Every minute for him was an exhilarating one.

The branding went on for a week. About five hundred cattle were branded daily, and William worked steadily with the men. Unlike his father, he neither smelled the stench nor heard the rough language. Instead, he saw only miles and miles of green prairie, thousands of cattle, horses that were smart and well trained, and cowboys who had developed to the highest degree the art of riding, roping, and cutting; and, as he watched, he dreamed his own dream of the future.

The foreman in charge of the outfit was a small, wiry man whose name, Red Williams, was suggested by the color of his hair. Several of the trail-driving outfit had agreed to stay on with the Half Circle K, one of them a young Mexican. In the outfit were some ten or fifteen men. Red, Art Sherrod, and Fred Patchin had been part of the Bar O outfit when Koogle bought the Bar O Ranch from Sacra and Sugg. Red had been the range boss. Having worked on the ranch since its establishment, they preferred staying on to moving back to the Indian Territory with their former employer. Fred, who was known as the Bar O Kid, was the bronc buster. He was a tall, thin, young man, not too many years older than William. Among the others were Pat Gormley, Barr Brown, Dave Buchanan, Don Blaylock, Ed Johnson, Sam Hitson, Clint Phillips, Boney the cook, Billy Freeman, and the boys from South Texas.

From the day of William's arrival at the ranch, the cowboy who attracted him most was the Negro, Billy Freeman. Billy Freeman, before moving to Texas with some southern family, had been a jockey. As a result, he was by far the outfit's most expert rider. William watched with fascination as he pursued and roped a recalcitrant calf, his body in perfect motion with that of the horse. William was fully aware that a top cowboy had to be, first of all, an expert roper, for the occasions were numerous when only a rope could get the job done effectively, and he determined that in the future he would use every spare minute to practice with his lariat on horseback. He realized that he must acquire by himself the many kinds of knowledge every cowboy had but never passed on to a beginner: how to sit in the saddle as if he and his mount were one; how to hold his position firmly by the pressure of his knees; how to give directions by the handling of the reins; and, of greater importance, how to swing that long loop over his shoulder and out at exactly the right moment. William never tired of watching the Negro whom he had chosen as his model.

The pony Billy rode most of the time was his own, a small but stoutly built animal with a short head, short ears, and much width between the eyes. Evidently it was not its appearance that made the pony valuable, but its smart and docile ways, its surefootedness, and its zest for chasing cattle. William enjoyed most watching the way the horse stopped in its tracks the moment it felt the jerk of the rope that threw the calf, or the ease with which it lowered its hock to pivot on its hind legs into a reverse direction when the calf suddenly turned round.

After Billy Freeman, William liked best to watch the young Mexican from South Texas, not because of the Mexican himself, although he, too, was an expert rider, but because of his unusual saddle. In the manner of all Western saddles, it was deep seated and had a horn sufficiently strong to hold the heaviest steer; it had other features as well, chief among which were wide wooden stirrups enclosed with a piece of leather, which the Mexican said was called a *tapadero*. There would never be any need for boots if you had a saddle like that, William thought.

Because William was the son of one of the owners of the ranch and the little Negro Birl was not only lonely and far from home but too young to have the respect of the other hands, the two boys became fast friends and formed a defensive comradeship quite outside the inner circle of cowboys. By the end of the week, William had learned every detail of the cattle drive from South Texas and of the way in which Birl had become part of the Tandy outfit.

The two stories William told on his return home were not given full credence by either of his parents until later when time had proved them not to be youthful exaggerations. The Tandy herd was supposedly a herd of steers. In purchasing them, Koogle also agreed to take several hundred cows, for which he paid a higher than usual price—fourteen dollars a head—because they all had calves. With characteristic carelessness, he failed to send a man of his own to join the Tandy outfit as they trailed the herd northward for delivery. Unfortunately, the Tandy foreman was neither a competent trail driver nor a man of integrity. Upon reaching the railroad, he cut out all the yearling calves and, with the help of an accomplice who rebranded them, shipped them to market. Little care was given the cattle on the drive. As a result, many of the baby calves had not survived the trip. By the time the herd reached the Panhandle, over half the calves were gone. The profit from the entire transaction had been wiped out long before the cattle were received.

As for Birl's story,[1] the outfit on going through Tyler had passed a group of Negro children playing in a road on the outskirts of town. Having never before seen so numerous a number of grotesque-looking animals together, the children followed along, scampering, and playing at a safe distance behind. After a while, a man on horse-

---

[1] Willie Newbury Lewis, *Between Sun and Sod* (Clarendon: Clarendon Press, 1938), p. 145.

back stopped to inquire if any of the boys wanted to take a ride. Since the stranger was pleasant looking and the invitation inviting, Birl accepted.

"Don't git in a hurry," the stranger said. "We've got to wait till the chuck wagon gits here."

Very shortly, it came lumbering around the bend in the road. Driving the team was a Negro man who, Birl quickly learned, went by the name of Boze and cooked for the outfit.

There was a short, mumbled conversation between the two men, after which the mounted man stooped down, picked Birl up, and placed him on the seat beside the driver. As he rode away, he shouted instructions to buy the boy candy and fruit at the next town. Boze was friendly, and the candy and fruit were delicacies with which the boy was rarely favored; so for a time he rode happily on, engrossed with the adventure.

By sundown, however, he grew weary and wanted to go home. On finding his frequent requests to be returned to Tyler ignored, he began to cry. Boze attempted to soothe him, but, failing that, took a bottle from his pocket, and forced a large mouthful of its contents down Birl's throat. It was well into the morning of another day before the boy awakened from his drunken stupor. When he began again to whimper, Boze assured him that the wagon had been turned around and was on its way back to Tyler. He learned eventually that this was not true, but by that time he had realized there was nothing he could do; furthermore, his new life was proving more adventurous than anything he had ever before experienced, and gradually, as the days went by, he ceased to pine for his family and playmates.

Immediately after turning over the cattle to their new owner, the Tandy foreman and Boze, together with the cowboys who had not joined the Half Circle K outfit, departed without a word of farewell or explanation to the little Negro they left behind.

When William's mother asked her brother why he had become a party to a kidnapping, he laughed and replied, "I suppose you are partly correct. In buying him from the rascals, I was a sort of accomplice. But let's look at it another way. I could see he was a good kid, and Carrie is in sore need of someone to help her with the work. We are prepared to give him a good home till he is grown. Do you think he would have fared any better had I let him go on with those men?"

In time, being more of a realist than a moralist, she came to agree. William's father, on the other hand, could never be made to understand. For him, the code of a man of honor was clearly defined. Mitigating circumstances were of little consequence. Furthermore, he was possibly more critical of his brother-in-law than he would have been of another, for, as William knew well, his uncle was the personification of all the things his father found most distasteful in the West.

CHAPTER XI

On reaching home, William was distressed to find that one of his cows was ailing. Already she was too weak to stand, and her urine was discolored by the presence of blood. Having no familiarity with the diseases of cattle, he hastened out to Parson Allen's to learn from him, if possible, the nature of the illness and a remedy, if there was one.

Allen, on hearing the symptoms, shook his head and said, "There's nothing you can do. It's tick fever, that's what it is, carried in by that blasted herd the Hearts brought up from the south country a few weeks ago. Do you know that most of the old scrawny things that carried the ticks in are fine, but all my fat cows are either dead or dying? You'll lose all of yours and your mother's milk cows, too, for they are the kind that seem to get it quickest and die the fastest."

Allen's predictions were correct. One by one all the cows in the corral sickened and died. It was a real catastrophe for William. Not only had he worked all summer, but also he had made the arduous hunt for the stray mules all alone to earn some money. In spite of his keen disappointment, he was comforted a little by a feeling that there were sometimes circumstances over which an individual had no control. His confidence in his ability to become a cowboy and have a herd of his own remained unshaken. He would simply have to work harder to make up for his loss.

Even with their disappointments and frustrations, the summer and fall had been a full and happy period for him. Because of the encroaching drought, the grasses were dry and brown, but the cottonwoods along the creek were sporting their autumn gold, and the shinnery made patches of dark red on the landscape. There was no school in the colony that winter, since there were so few pupils. On days when he failed to get employment, William mounted Tex and rode away, sometimes to Saddler to bag for dinner one of the hundreds of wild turkeys that roosted in the trees and fed close to the creek banks, sometimes to Bushey to watch the birds. Quail were abundant, and the cheerful, staccato whistle of the bobwhite charmed him. It was seldom that he raised his gun to shoot into a covey. It amused him to sit astride his horse as the birds rose in a whirr at the sound of Tex's hoofbeats, then as quickly lit again when the danger seemed no longer there. But he liked most to watch them after sundown as they took their places to squat in a large circle, sometimes forty babies strong, with tails in and heads out, while the father of the covey stood guard at the side.

On most days, however, he worked in his father's store or did any odd job that came to hand. Even he realized that his months in Clarendon were already showing their effects in many ways. His naturally fair skin, which, together with his blue eyes, had once given him an almost effeminate appearance, still had the tan he had first acquired on the surveying trip. He was proud of the inches he had added to his height, and he felt certain that everyone must know by now that he acted and felt much older than his approaching sixteen years. He was no longer William, but Billy, to all except his mother, his father, his sister, and himself. He agreed with Satterwhite that his name was not suitable for a cowboy, but he had been called William too long to think of himself by any other name.

One morning as he was passing Corbett's lean-to, he noticed a large cottonwood log extending out the front door, across the walk, and into the street. When he stopped to look, he was joined by Will Murdock, who was on one of his rare visits to town.

"Well, I see winter has come," Will said. "From now on everyone who goes to town will have the fun of jumping Corbett's log."

"Jumping his log?" inquired William.

"Yes, jumping his log. It's a mean job to cut down a cottonwood and get it into town, and the old man says that it takes so much of his time that there is none left to saw it up into the proper size for the stove. It's simpler to put one end in and push in the rest gradually as it burns down."

William thought it a great joke, but it also gave him an idea. On the way home after work, he stopped, as he often did, to chat a few minutes with Corbett. He was a good, old man, apparently without either family or friends, and William's sympathy went out to him. This visit, however, was a matter of business. Before he left, the two had reached an agreement by which the cobbler would be kept in firewood. All winter, in a rickety wagon that had once belonged to his uncle, William drove periodically to the creek, felled a tree, cut it into stove lengths, and stacked the logs close to the back door of the lean-to. The job paid very little, but it was steady work.

It was, however, not a winter of all work and no play. Every effort was made by the better class of settlers to make life in the colony as nearly normal as was possible in an isolated frontier town. Even though the saloon occupied the church building, services were held every Sunday. When the Reverend Mr. Cooper was not in Mobeetie they were held at the home of Judge White. Mrs. White had an organ. On those days Will Murdock rang the bell loudly and well in advance. The parlor was always filled, for the social aspect of the gathering appealed even to those who lacked interest in morals and theology. When Cooper preached, the little minister taught Methodism as vehemently as he had directed the unloading of the piano, but with less colorful language. The Negro Birl was often present, although his Catholic mistress, Koogle's wife, was forbidden by church law to attend a Protestant service.

CHAPTER XII

In simple ways such as this, the days and months passed. With the approach of Thanksgiving, the family drove out to the J. A. Ranch to spend the holiday weekend with Goodnight and Mollie. William's father was hesitant to accept the hospitality of a man for whom he had little regard, but his curiosity to see the ranch and his family's eagerness prevailed. The drive was pleasant; even on the plains, fall was a beautiful time of year in the Panhandle. The heat and scorching sun were gone, and the air had, at once, an invigorating coolness and a caressing warmth. It was sundown before the hack turned into the long lane that led to the house.

It was the family's first experience on a well-established free grass ranch. To the newcomers, it was like a feudal domain. The log cabin originally occupied by Goodnight and his wife had been replaced by a large, frame cottage. The cabin had been turned over to the ranch manager and his family. Besides these two structures there was the messhouse, which, although partly dugout and partly rock, was of a size to accommodate the thirty or forty hands that came and went between headquarters and outlying camps. At one side stood the corral and the two chuck wagons used during the spring and summer work.

The broad strip of land that led to the house passed between two pastures. To the right was a field of grain. In the fenced pasture on the left grazed a herd of buffalo. At the end of the lane was the huge gate that opened into the headquarters' enclosure. The fence around the buffalo pasture was of cedar logs and barbed wire, but the one around the buildings was of planks with a wide plank on top. The cowboys were in for supper, and across the top rail of the fence rested their saddles neatly side by side. Way down at the end, "jerky"—strips of beef—was hung out to dry. Behind the houses rose a high hill, like a mother nestling her young against her bosom.

The visit was a time of delight for William. From sunup until sundown every day, in company with the manager's sons, Crockett and Henry, he roamed the adjacent prairies, sometimes on foot, sometimes on horseback. It was fun to holler and tease the buffalo into rushing them, then, at the last minute, to scramble to safety under the fence. It was like a game to scan the ground for the telltale track of a passing lobo, a track that resembled so closely a human hand with claws for fingers, and to hear Crockett tell how that wily animal managed to down a big steer by biting a tendon of his hind leg at a place that crippled him.

One day when the earth was warm from the noon sun, they saw a big rattler, still numb from the chill of the previous night, slither slowly across the road. After many long-distance attempts, Crockett landed a rock on its head, pinning it to the ground. William watched, with both fear and fascination, as the angered snake thrashed its jingling tail until death stopped it.

Late in the afternoon of the fourth day while they were unsaddling after a long ride, a cowboy rode up and, without stopping to tie his horse, hastened into the house. In a few minutes he came out again, accompanied by Goodnight.

On noticing the boys, Goodnight called to them, "Some Indians are coming. The fellow that spotted them says they are Comanches, and Comanches are the biggest liars and cheats, and the most ferocious fighters on the plains. But don't be alarmed. All they want here is a big buffalo, the lazy good-for-nothings that they are."

He had no sooner finished speaking than the hunting party came into view. They were a motley aggregation, like the band William had been frightened by during his trip after Gatherin's mules. The men were bedecked in as much of their warrior trappings as had survived their semi-imprisonment on the reservation. Their braided and straggling hair held a feather or two, and a few had painted their bodies gaudily above the waist. Some wore moccasins, while others had added to the incongruity of their costumes army issue shoes and trousers. All carried either an old buffalo robe or an army blanket as protection against the cold.

Goodnight, who was provoked, shouted in a peremptory tone of voice, "Move on, you scurvy beggars. There's nothing for you around this part of the world."

The band stopped and waited as a lone Indian, evidently the leader of the party, rode slowly toward the house. As he drew near,

William was surprised to see that he had a stern but intelligent face and was a man of fine physique.

On reaching Goodnight, he pointed toward Mrs. Goodnight and, with coolness and dignity spoke. "Squaw sick. Must have buffalo to make medicine."

Goodnight shook his head, but to all his continued refusals the chief turned a deaf ear. Only once did he threaten Goodnight by saying that, if he were not given a buffalo, he would cause a storm to come. Finally, as dusk came on, Goodnight agreed to let the party camp on the ranch overnight and to provide them with food from the commissary. Temporarily appeased, they pitched their tents, ate, and peaceably enough retired.

At daylight, however, they were again at the house repeating their demands of the previous evening, with Goodnight still adamant. As the argument continued, the clatter of hoof beats announced the arrival of a group of soldiers. On drawing near, the sergeant in charge dismounted and approached Goodnight. The Indians, it seems, had run away from the Indian Territory in the hope of reaching New Mexico and freedom. It was the business of the soldiers to make certain their return to the reservation. This could, of course, be achieved by force, but it would be better for all concerned if a more peaceful means could be found. If the Indians were given the buffalo they wanted so badly, the soldier felt certain he would have no further trouble in getting them to go back.

Goodnight readily agreed to the soldier's proposal, and as soon as permission to kill the buffalo was given, one Indian alone rode into the herd. The others stood around patiently as he cut out his buffalo and rode out of sight. When he and the animal disappeared from view, the remainder mounted in a body to follow. Having achieved the object of their hunt and satisfied their needs, they were ready to return to their reservation. They willingly started back with the soldiers.

It may have been the presence of the Indians that aroused in Goodnight memories of certain periods in his past—of his boyhood in South Texas and his experiences as a frontier scout and ranger. He began to talk as soon as they all were comfortably settled in the parlor after supper one night and continued on for hours after the women had retired to their rooms. As the story of the founding and development of the ranch unfolded, William began to identify himself with the speaker till, at the end, it was not the man who was talking, it was William himself who was lord of a domain thirty-five miles square, with camps at every strategic point, and a thirty-man outfit, many of whom handled a gun as well as they handled horses and cattle.

"You must remember, Lewis," Goodnight concluded, "that a large part of the Panhandle still belongs to the state, and if some equitable agreement about leasing cannot be reached soon, the cattleman is doomed. Everything you and I have worked for and accomplished will soon be lost."

The following morning William accompanied the two men as they rode over to inspect a special bunch of cattle in an adjacent pasture.

"They are a new breed here," said the owner of the ranch, "called Hereford. They are not only of a much finer appearance, but they will supposedly produce heavier beef. I now have some bulls and about four hundred head of cows. If they do as well as I expect, I may soon own the finest range cattle in the country."

It was still early morning. To the right of the pasture gate was a small hillock. On it were one hundred or so calves, the most beautiful the boy had ever seen. Their brown curly-haired bodies glistened in the sun as they turned their white faces in unison to watch the movements of the visitors.

"Notice the one cow grazing near the calves," said Goodnight. "She has been left behind to stand guard while the other mothers go to water. Another one will do duty tomorrow."

After supper that evening the subject of free grass and leasing arose, and again the men talked far into the night. The dispute over legal possession of ranges heretofore held by right of possession was becoming a matter of much controversy between cattlemen and lawmakers. Although much of the conversation was on subjects beyond his full understanding, William sat spellbound. It was the Panhandle they were describing, and the Panhandle was to be his home for the remainder of his life. He was certain of that.

With keen interest, he listened as Goodnight continued, "Very few people, even in Texas, know anything about this part of the state. It is an unsettled region, far removed from the state's governing body," and he went on to explain that, as a result, laws engendered by the needs of more advanced and better understood districts were often not advantageous to the plains country. Furthermore, an unusual condition existed: the division of the territory into counties with local courts had only recently been undertaken. Donley County itself had been organized only a few years before in 1882. In the absence of recognized law and order, another kind of authority had arisen. In many cases the land was held—either by ownership, custom, or force—in large blocks by individuals whose employees were fighting men as well as cowhands. Each separate outfit, fortified by its own organized personnel, became almost a law unto itself capable of protecting both collective and individual interests without outside assistance.

As the settlers of less power and property increased in number, a more established procedure was necessary to protect their rights. When Donley was organized, Clarendon was made the county seat, and a more orthodox method of law enforcement was attempted. So far, however, it had commanded respect neither from its administrators nor from its supposed beneficiaries and was, therefore, laxly enforced. The judicial body itself was composed of men with the same pioneer temperament; otherwise, they would not have been elected to office. Being of the same temperament as the early cattlemen, they had an understanding of the people and the land and were activated by motives that often did not coincide with the objectives of laws made by less sympathetic politicians. Together with the cattlemen they became engaged in a conflict far greater than a mere struggle for the land. It was the spiritual conflict of two opposing cultures: the one evolving from the freedom of the open spaces and the power produced by the possession of a fleet horse and a gun; the other from the gentler background of forest, field, and stream, recognized traditions, group living, and respect for authority. In time, William was to recognize the fact that his uncle represented the one, and his father the other.

In 1881, the first of the many laws introduced to prevent the holding of large blocks of land was passed. By this Seven Section Act[1] a settler was privileged to acquire at a nominal cost seven sections of land; the only stipulations were that he erect a dwelling of sorts, sleep a required number of nights in the dwelling, and put a certain number of acres under cultivation during the tentative ownership period.

The law did not, however, always serve its intended purpose of protecting the small landholder for it was this very law that made possible Koogle's acquisition of the choice sections upon which he built. These sections possessed the last living water until the subsidiary creeks of the Canadian were reached. Through legal ownership of this water he came, along with Goodnight and the Diamond F Ranch, into control of countless acres of free range. Without water the free range was useless to anyone else.

At the same time that the first lease law was passed, another law came into being: this one directed at preventing the usage without fee of state-owned land. This law, known as the Enclosure Act, forbade the enclosure of the public domain without an annual leasing payment of four cents per acre. Because of this law, Koogle built his drift fence in a manner which, up to this point, had obviated the payment of the lease. It was not the money involved, for it was a negligible amount, but the principle, that aroused the ire of the cattlemen. Firm in the belief that the land was of no value except for grazing purposes and that the state had no right to demand payment on something that was already theirs by possession, all the stockmen continued to disregard the law.

After several years of failure to enforce the act, the legislature resolved not only to raise the price to eight cents per acre, but to make it a misdemeanor to appropriate land without payment. All through the summer and fall of 1885, men scoffingly called grass commissioners roamed the Panhandle in search of violators. Meanwhile, the more intelligent cattlemen, having come to realize that the course

---

[1] The Seven Section Act was a term used for the Sales Act Amendment of 1881 by the ranchers and farmers of the Panhandle. It referred in particular to section 5 of the 1881 bill. See Sales Act §5, as amended, Tex. Laws 1881, ch. 105 at 120, 9 Gammel, Laws of Texas 212 (1898).

of progress and change was inevitable, agreed among themselves to pay the lease provided the legislators would return to their original demand of four cents only. Goodnight was sent to Austin as their spokesman. The opposition was adamant, and once again no settlement was reached. Goodnight had returned from the capital only a few days before William and his parents arrived at the J. A. Ranch for their weekend visit.

On the day of their departure, as William's family stepped into the buggy to return home, their host said with a shake of his big head, "It is most unfortunate that I was unable to make those mules in Austin understand the state of affairs in the Panhandle. The name of everyone we know is on the list of violators, yours among them, and mine is at the head. Unless I miss my guess, we'll all come to trial sometime next year. If that happens, there will arise the most ludicrous situation in the history of this part of the world. I am foreman of the grand jury that will be forced to make the indictments. A misdemeanor cannot be tried except in the county where it occurred. There are not more than seventy men in the county eligible for jury duty, and, with the exception of the merchant, the doctor, the preacher, and Judge White, everyone of them either owns cattle or works on a ranch. What do you think will happen when the state's attorney pleads his case before a bunch of 'tried and true' men such as that? Anyway, it will be a great show."

CHAPTER XIII

Christmas came. William and the Stocking boys brought a large cedar in from the breaks, setting it up in the saloon that had been temporarily cleared for the occasion. For days William and the two "socks" strung into garlands the popped corn and cranberries Rosie had freighted in for the purpose.

Everyone from near and far was present on Christmas night for a general exchange of presents. In the absence of Carrie, Koogle sat with the boys from his outfit. Carrie and William's mother had remained at the house to nurse the newly born baby who seemed to be ailing. When it was the little Negro boy's time to receive a gift, he was embarrassed to find a package containing a squirming object placed in his hand.

"Open it quickly," William said.

A small, black puppy wriggled out to the delight of the audience.

"Hurrah!" shouted one of the Half Circle K boys.

Everyone applauded, and the fun went on.[1]

Two weeks later Carrie's baby died. Because William was the youngest member of the family, it became his duty to make most of the funeral arrangements. He got a carpenter to make the tiny casket. He wielded the hammer for Vashti Parks and Sella Gentry as they lined the box with a blanket and a Paisley shawl Mrs. Parks had brought from New Mexico. Because there was no priest available, the Reverend Mr. Cooper was asked to officiate at the funeral. It was William who explained to him that his aunt was a devout Catholic and would not feel that her baby had been properly buried unless a Hail, Mary and a Glory be to the Father were said along with the Methodist service. It was something the minister preferred not doing, but his sympathy for the bereaved mother overcame his religious objections and he acquiesced.

There was no hearse in town, and a hack had to be used as a substitute. Halfway up the incline to the flat above the river, the horses balked—an unfortunate incident that made it necessary for William and his father to carry the box by hand the remainder of the way.

It was 7 January 1886, and the day was as sunny and warm as a day in spring. Not one cloud broke the wide expanse of blue sky. It was late afternoon before Cooper began the Lord's Prayer. During the service an ominous dark bank arose on the northern horizon. A wind from the same direction blew in a few scattered clouds, then subsided as quickly as it had come, leaving the atmosphere sultry and still, as still as if even the earth had stopped moving. Before the minister finished his prayer, the norther struck. By the time the grave was filled, the sky was completely overcast; it was as dark as late dusk, and the sudden, cold wind had turned into a freezing gale. It

---

[1] Willie Newbury Lewis, *Between Sun and Sod* (Clarendon: Clarendon Press, 1938), p. 177.

was night when the family reached home, and the air was filled with stinging and whirling particles of ice and snow.

All night the wind raged, and the house creaked as if it would collapse under the next blast. Steadily, until the following afternoon, the snow continued to fall, so thick and fast that it was impossible to see two feet ahead. William sat up, wrapped in blankets, to assure the stove's being kept red hot. It was the onset of the worst blizzard in the history of the Panhandle.

On the first day that the ground was passable, Koogle and William's father drove out upon the plains to estimate the damage. Because the buckboard, which they used in preference to the heavier hack, seated only two comfortably, William, who was eager to go along, rode Tex. Sickening sights greeted them. For the entire length of one drift fence, cattle lay in piles so high it would have been possible to walk for a long distance on top of them without touching a foot to the ground. Instinct had forced the dumb creatures to move away from the wind, and they had drifted until stopped by the barrier of barbed wire. Presumably, they had huddled there in bewilderment, bellowing mournfully until they froze stiff. Koogle and William's father knew that the same condition existed at the other fences even though they did not drive that far. The few cattle that survived were those which were in the canyons where snow-covered brush and mesquite trees had not only protected them in a measure from the cold, but also had provided them with temporary fodder until the snow disappeared from the grass.

The catastrophe left the smaller ranchmen bankrupt. They had no herds, only a few horses for which they no longer had any use. The large companies were severely injured. The Quarter Circle Heart lost over five hundred cattle in one corner west of town. Many steers, in an effort to reach brush, had stepped off into snow-filled crevices of the cap rock. It was a crippling blow for the three partners of the Half Circle K.

During the disheartening weeks that followed the blizzard and the death of her baby, Carrie did not speak. She also refused to return to the ranch. One morning toward the end of January, Koogle placed his wife and small son on the stage for Fort Worth and home.

"I wonder if it would not be better for her if she never returned," William's mother remarked to William's father and her children, as they sat around the living room table discussing the events of the last few weeks. "She does not possess the kind of spiritual timber necessary for a woman to survive the rigors of the frontier. Nor is my brother the kind of protector necessary for one of so gentle a nature."

"Don't blame him too harshly," William's father interposed. "He would not intentionally harm anyone, but he should never have married, for he is still an adventurer at heart and a willing prey to his weaknesses."

After several weeks Carrie did return. However, during the following two years she spent much of her time in Kansas City.

CHAPTER XIV

In April 1886 William moved to the ranch to work until late fall. Since the spring rounding and branding were under way, only a few of the outfit were at headquarters on the day he arrived. As he alighted from his mount and untied his bedroll, he wondered if the men whose talents he admired so extravagantly were going to look with scorn upon him and his ignorance. He was on familiar terms with much of the country and the feel of a horse, it was true, but it required less skill to ride old Tex than to cut out cows or break broncs. He was going to learn, he swore to himself, and nothing was going to stop him.

While he was unsaddling, the foreman walked over toward him. With no greeting other than a wave of his hand toward the place from which he had emerged, he said testily, "Throw your things in there with the boys, not in the house, and remember you are not on a visit to your uncle this time."

William recognized the hostility of his tone. "He doesn't like me because I am the son of one of the owners," he thought, "but it won't make any difference. I'll work just like all the rest."

Red Williams, the foreman, was a small man. He weighed only

110 pounds but possessed a drive that more than offset any impression of frailty his appearance might have given. This enabled him to dominate men twice his size. He was a man without fear, and heat, cold, thirst, and hunger had little effect on him.

On the evening after William's arrival, Red boasted to another one of the men, "I'll punish him so hard he'll have to give up and go back to town where he belongs. Who in the hell wants to be bothered with a tenderfoot kid?" William was soon told about it by one of the hands.

He had been at headquarters about four days when Red informed him that all the boys, including the cook and Birl, were to leave the following morning to be away for a while.

"You'll have to stay behind," he said sarcastically, "to see that all the school children around here don't steal anything. Your uncle sure would hate that, wouldn't he?"

It angered William, but he answered only that he would even though he knew there was not even a school in Clarendon.

At the coming of daylight the outfit left. The lonely boy, heartsick and disappointed, watched until the lumbering wagon and the riders had disappeared over the farthest rise. He was alone for how long he did not know, and the loneliness was hard to endure. There were plenty of provisions, but he had no knowledge of cookery. It was only after many attempts that he managed to boil his beans to an edible stage without scorching them or to broil his bacon without burning it to a crisp. The art of making biscuit he was unable to master. He enjoyed reading, but the books were in the main house. No one was in the house, and he had no key. He looked longingly at the broncs grazing in the adjoining pasture, for he would have liked to try to ride one when there was no one to watch. He knew, however, that he could neither catch nor mount one without help. So day after day he saddled Tex—to have something alive to talk to as much as to ride—and wandered over the rolling plains, but always within easy distance of the house. As sundown approached, he went to the lake for a swim, then into the bunkhouse for the night. He thought once of going home for a good meal, but quickly rejected the idea. He must not give Red the satisfaction of thinking he had objected to any part of his sojourn alone at headquarters. He was on proving ground, and he knew it.

At the end of the second week the outfit returned. The foreman did not inquire how he had managed, and William volunteered no information. It was as if the incident had never occurred except for the unusual friendliness of the older hands. Their ready acceptance of him was a reward he had not anticipated. He felt amply repaid for his two weeks of loneliness.

Whenever Koogle's family was in Kansas City, he had no use for the Negro boy and placed him in the hands of the cook. It was Birl who became William's companion in misery. For both of them the foreman exhibited a strong antipathy. His dislike of the colored boy appeared to be without ground. His dislike of himself, William felt, was more easily understood. Because he was a rough and unlettered man, it offended him personally for a well-mannered youth from a background of education and culture to presume that he, too, was capable of performing what Red termed "a man's work."

To make their life more unbearable, Red never allowed the boys to ride anywhere with the men. If there were a particularly unpleasant job to be done, it always fell to their lot to do it. The first real work assigned them was to clean the river, an odious chore that the majority of the men would have refused to do. The Salt Fork ran a diagonal course across Koogle's sections. In it hundreds of cattle that had not succumbed during the first days of the big freeze, had finally perished as they milled around over the frozen riverbed in an effort to get to water. Their bloated bodies, the legs held stiff in the air, made a repulsive sight. The stench from their rotting flesh fouled the atmosphere for a quarter of a mile. To tie a dead cow to the saddle horn, then drag it out was both a strenuous and a nauseating job. William was often forced to dismount because of his need to vomit. Day after day the two boys labored until ordered to stop. Their efforts had done little toward cleaning the river, but the severity of the experience had evidently satisfied Red.

There followed a short respite in which they were given such simple tasks as rustling the horses in the morning, gathering wood, or heating the branding irons. One morning, they rode in with the *remuda* while the outfit was still at breakfast. Among the horses was a gray pony that Red wanted broken for his string before the start of the big roundup. Because the animal was fractious and continued to pitch at the touch of the saddle, Fred, the bronc buster, had postponed working with the pony until after he had finished with the more tractable horses. On that morning, as William walked toward the messhouse, he heard the bronc buster say to Red, "I'm not goin' to ride that horse for you today. I'll have him ready by the time you want him. If you're in such an all-fired hurry, get up on him yourself."

Red answered, "I'll get up on him all right, but"—and he laughed—"not until after he has worn himself down a little with someone else. I'll put the little nigger on him for a while."

"You wouldn't do that, would you?" Fred protested. "That's a real mean horse. Handling him will take someone that knows how. You could kill that boy."

Red only shrugged. "That wouldn't matter too much. I'd just tell the old man a horse kicked him in the head, and he wouldn't care. He don't know what to do with him anyway while his wife and kid are away."

Fred was not a mean man and would never have done to a helpless child what Red was preparing to do. However, he was young and liked his job. He had opposed the foreman once that day, and he clearly felt that it would not be wise to do it again. Although an unwilling party, he helped Red saddle and hold the bronc while the Negro boy, too terrified to voice an objection, was lifted onto the horse. To prevent the saddle's slipping sideways, the men tied Birl's feet underneath the horse's belly. Then, with a shout and a slap, they turned him loose.

Before William's unbelieving eyes, the bronc went up into the air and back down again, back hunched and forelegs stiff as they hit the ground, in a movement that snapped his rider like the crack of a whip. Up, then down again, till the little Negro was no longer able to hold his head erect. With each successive thud, blood oozed from his nose.

After a few minutes Fred reached for his rope, turning as he did so, to say to the foreman, "Bronc ridin' is my job. I'm not too good a roper, and you know it, but I'm goin' to stop that horse if it's the last thing I ever do. The nigger boy could be killed anyway, but it's the only thing left that might save his life."

Meanwhile, on hearing the commotion, the other cowboys came out to learn the cause of it. As Fred was talking and preparing to throw, another rope went through the air. William turned and saw that it was the Mexican boy who had thrown it. The pony reared to a sudden stop, lassoed around the neck, and stumbled, but, as good fortune would have it, did not fall. After the Mexican, whose expert roping had saved the boy, untied him to hand him to Boney, he turned to villify Red in a stream of foreign words. The language was not understood, but its meaning was clear. Birl had acquired a new friend and an ally.

The injured Birl was placed in Boney's hands. The cook put him to bed and gave him enough whiskey to soothe him. Good old man that Boney was, he sat beside the boy all through the day and the night, rubbing the soreness from his wracked muscles and talking in an effort to allay his terror. In due time, Birl recovered. No member of the outfit ever alluded to the incident. A week later the two boys were sent to the camp on the Boggy.

The Boggy, a small tributary of Allen Creek, was a stream where cattle often had trouble. It was a common practice, at that time, to ride the creeks in the spring to rescue any cattle that had become bogged. In dry seasons, such as the spring of 1886, the measures had to be doubled. It was for this reason that William and Birl had been ordered to the Boggy. There had been no rain during the late summer months of the previous year. In many of the creeks the streams no longer ran, and the only water to be found in them was contained in muddy holes with a wide, muddy edge extending all around them. As the water diminished, the surrounding mud acquired a quicksand quality that held in a vise-like grip anything that got into it. Only the strongest of animals were able to struggle free without assistance. Adding to the difficulty was the weakened condition of the cows. The range grasses, so dependent on seasonal rains, were thin and lacking in nutritious value, and the cows that had been turned out to winter on them were in a correspondingly poor condition. Driven to desperation by the heel fly, which always abounded at that time of year, the senseless and undernourished creatures sought relief in the only refuge offered by nature, a stream or a water hole.

The Boggy was particularly troublesome, not only because of its numerous holes, but also because the banks on either side rose to a height of six or eight feet, causing the cow to sink deeper than usual when she jumped. This also added to the difficulties of the rescue. For two weeks William and Birl rode up and down the creek, roping imprisoned cattle and extricating them by means of a lariat and the strength of their horses. Besides the ample provisions with which Boney had supplied them, there was a log cabin of sorts that Sugg had thrown together for the convenience of his bog riders. Since both of the boys were young, they found one another companionable. The two weeks passed quickly and without mishap. By the time they were called back to camp, preparations were well under way for the big roundup.

CHAPTER XV

Extending all the way up through the center and into the western part of the Panhandle was an unenclosed area of many miles. Being plains country, it was covered with a short but drought-resistant grass called mesquite. Upon these free and ordinarily nutritious grasslands, the stockmen turned their herds loose in the fall to graze through the winter. The cattle, as they grazed, drifted away from the wind. During severe storms they drifted far and wide. It was this drifting that necessitated a combined effort of rounding each year—the big roundup, as it was called.

Roundup was an operation of considerable magnitude, involving numerous ranches, their wagons, hands, and horses. The objective of this pool outfit was to gather and return to their home ranges the scattered herds. The area to be covered extended from the Salt Fork to above the Canadian River valley, and from the interior of the Indian Territory to Fort Sumner on the west. Every major outfit sent a wagon, with the smaller operators represented by one or two of their cowboys. Each of these "stray" men, as they were called, and his string of cow ponies was attached to a certain wagon, to work under orders as one of the hands as long as he remained with the roundup.

The Half Circle K wagon was to start from Clarendon. On the day before the scheduled departure, the cowboys rode into town to assist in loading, and also to purchase any necessary additional clothing and to enjoy the luxury of a barbershop shave and the pleasures of the saloon. William went straight home to visit with his parents before repacking his bedroll and returning to work with Boney. As an added touch of malice on the part of the foreman, William and Birl had been assigned to the cook. Their job was to help in making camp, to stake the horses, and to take turns riding behind the *remuda* and in the wagon. William was partially aware, himself, that he would have resented Red's attitude had he had more time to dwell on it, but he was too excited. He felt he was on the threshold of what might well be the greatest adventure of his life. So long as he had the privilege of taking an active part in the roundup, his particular role was of little consequence.

Before him stood the lumbering wagon that was to be the center of his existence for the next two months. All afternoon he worked enthusiastically with Boney, stretching the great sheets over the bows, filling the water barrel, and securing it according to instructions, with the faucet turned outward, packing in each bedroll and slicker as each was passed to him, and chopping wood from the creek into the proper length to fit with ease into the rawhide that was loosely stretched between the undersides of the wagon bed. The chuck box, baking oven, and skillets had already been put carefully in their places by the cook.

"Throw in the snatch chain and ax," Boney shouted when William came up with his final armful of wood, "and we'll be ready to roll in the morning."

As William turned to leave, he saw his uncle ride in. It was the first time he had seen him in several weeks. Koogle's continued absence from the ranch was something William had often wondered about. He must ask his father about it, he told himself. He hurried on his way, since the night before the beginning of the long drive was always the occasion for the ranch owner to give his outfit a big party. Although not a rancher on the scale of Goodnight, Rowe, and the Diamond F's, Bill Koogle was not the kind of man to be outdone by anyone. His outfit must have the best the town had to offer.

The festivities were in full swing long before William was dressed and back with the cowboys. A platform had been built behind the hotel. A table laden with various meats, cakes, and pies, all supplied by the local housewives, stood nearby. The cowboys were scrubbed till their faces shone, and dressed in the only suit and collar, usually celluloid, most of them owned. Since there were few women and girls in Clarendon, several cowboys, for the sake of taking part in the fun, tied a handkerchief around one arm and pretended to be of the opposite sex. Nearly everyone stepped onto the platform, at least once, to try his luck at dancing a polka or a schottische to a tune played by old Professor Combs on his homemade violin; afterwards, they feasted on food very unlike their customary bacon and beans.

Among the dancers William noticed two strangers. Unlike the other cowboys, they had not dressed for the occasion, but still wore chaps and colored shirts and had guns attached to their legs. All the cowboys carried Winchesters on their saddles, but few of them carried a gun. On the walk home William asked about the two strangers.

"They are Spur men," his father told him, "and will travel with the Half Circle K wagon. The drought has become so serious to the south of us that many ranch owners are moving their cattle out. These two were part of the outfit that brought the five thousand steers for us to pasture and will work with our boys as long as we keep the herd. I am not too happy over their presence. The part of the country they come from is filled with outlaws and cattle thieves. Consequently, most of the Spur boys are gunfighters, too. I suppose a gunfighter is necessary sometimes, but not on this kind of drive. It is my observation that an expert with a gun is too inclined to use it, whether the occasion demands it or not."

To William the prospect of traveling with professional gunmen only added to the excitement.

The wagon pulled out the following morning at daybreak. It was a thrilling sight for William: the huge canvas-covered vehicle with its double team; twelve cowboys, all in Stetsons, doeskins or leggins, boots, and colored shirts; and following them, the eighty or more horses that constituted the *remuda*. Behind them William came on Tex. He was aware that his mother was watching with anxious eyes as he rode off, almost as if he were leaving for good. Only his fear of appearing unmanly kept him from riding back to reassure her one more time.

At the Heart headquarters the outfit was joined by the Heart wagon. The R. O. was to be picked up next, and the other three as they traveled on. Some preliminary rounding was to be made before reaching the general assembling point near the Canadian River. Beyond the Heart pasture, where their route turned sharply to the east, the high plains extended for some fifteen miles in a narrow, finger-like ridge. From either side of this ridge many creeks flowed down to the prairies below, to form the Salt Fork on the south and both McClelland Creek and the North Fork of the Red River on the north. Bounded on two sides by the creeks, and on another by the Diamond F fence, was a large expanse of lush grassland, much prized as a winter pasture for cows. In the center was a good-sized lake. Since calves, unlike steers that drifted, tended to remain near the range where they were born, the work began in this pasture close to home. Part of the grassland was inside the Half Circle K fence. The remainder adjoined the Diamond F's, the R. O.'s, and the Heart's, and was used by all three of the ranches.

Long before sunup each morning, along with the smell of coffee and bacon, William was moving among the sleeping men, shouting with keen enjoyment, "Chuck away. Rise and shine, boys." While the cowboys finished breakfast, he and Birl were busy unstaking and getting into the rope corral the horses needed for the forenoon work.

Birl's experience on the bucking bronc made him lose all desire to ride horseback, and he never again mounted a horse unless necessity demanded it. William, on the contrary, enjoyed anything relating to horses. He not only liked them, as he liked all animals, but was eager to learn to handle them before Red forced him, as he had forced Birl, into a situation for which he was not yet prepared. He roped everything he saw. He was in the saddle at every opportunity, on anything available. He learned quickly, and he liked to think that he was one of the "born cowboys" described by Satterwhite on the stage drive from Harrold. Nevertheless, he was frequently thrown, for many of the broncs were not well broken. No one offered to help him. He was undertaking to master an art that had to be learned by the trial-and-error method. It could not be taught. He often went to bed too bruised and sore to sleep, but he was not discouraged. He had found the life he loved. He would learn.

His determination not only amused the other hands, especially the older ones, but aroused their admiration. It was not long before he discovered that a horse from the string of any one of them was always his when he needed a mount younger than Tex. Such indulgence, especially where he was concerned, William realized, was not looked upon with favor by Red. And presently Red's chance to "get at him" came.

A selection of horses, as was customary, had been made before leaving the ranch, with the men choosing in order of seniority. The selection was final, and, although an exchange between riders was permissible, if agreeable to both, it was rare. To allow someone to use a horse from his string was something Red would never have considered. As foreman, with first choice, he had the best working ponies and the most promising broncs on the ranch. Among them was a beautiful and intelligent roan, with some Spanish blood, as was often found in horses on the plains at the time. With the exception of Billy's pony, it was the smartest cutting pony in the *remuda*. By chance, it looked much like another roan that belonged to Dave Lyle, one of the two Spur men. One morning in the confusion of getting one horse out from the many fractious ones in the corral, William made the error of roping and saddling Red's horse for Dave.

Dave caught the mistake instantly, but in a spirit of devilment proceeded to mount. It would break the monotony of the morning to watch Red's performance on seeing another man, particularly one who did not belong to the Half Circle K outfit, on one of his horses. When the foreman finally noticed, his wrath was unbounded. He berated and villified both William and the cowboy. At first the Spur hand was amused, but as Red's furor increased, he, too, became riled. When he decided things had gone far enough, he jumped from his horse; but, before he had reached his adversary, bystanders rushed in between them. At no time must an argument be allowed to reach the fighting stage, particularly when one of the participants had as violent a temper as Red and the other was as quick on the draw as Dave. In time the belligerents regained enough of their composure to return to work, but Red remained angry with William.

There was only one roundup each day. In order to catch the mothers with their calves, it was begun very early in the morning. The branding followed the midday meal. If no mother could be established for a calf, it became a "maverick." The home brand of the ranch on which it was found, or if on free grass, the brand of the nearest ranch was run on the animal's side, and it became the rancher's property. A close record was kept during the branding.

As the last calf jumped from under the branding iron, the wagon wheels began to turn in the direction of the next pasture to be rounded. Progress was slow but steady. Grass everywhere was shorter than usual, from the dry and bitter seasons. Because the horses were thin, it was Red's intention to protect them as much as possible in the early stages of the long two months ahead. It was his aim each day to get to water by late afternoon, to let the cattle graze a while beforehand, then drink, after which they were content to bed down for the night. Water was necessary for the men as well as the animals. The barrel in the wagon held only an emergency supply, enough for the men for a short time only. So far, with the small operators eager to take their cattle home as quickly as gathered, the herd remained of a size that did not require a daytime stop for grazing. The horses grazed at night.

CHAPTER XVI

By the end of the week the pool outfit, complete with six wagons, had crossed into the Territory. The North Plains and the rough escarpment descent lay way behind. Rolling prairie was on all sides. Blue sage dotted the landscape. Wild grape, wild plum, and shin oak grew in profusion near the creeks. Low mountain ranges rose to the north and south. Nestled at their bases were the reservations of the Cheyenne and the Arapaho. The wagon's route lay directly between the two, as it circled into the interior, then out again, up toward the Canadian.

As the camp was struck on the first night, Red gave strict orders: "Keep a close watch on that *remuda*. There's nothing, except maybe whiskey, and a gun, that an Indian prizes as much as a horse. They'll use every means to steal one, in spite of you; and if they don't get it, the mustangs are liable to. Don't forget, either, that the boys in uniform speak for Uncle Sam. I don't know if they love Indians as much as they pretend, but they sure hate the guts of a cowboy. They don't even think he has the right to trail his herd across redskin country."

Notwithstanding the warning, all went well the first night and the following day. Very few cattle were located, which left the herd still small. The boys finished their supper on the second night and were returning their eating utensils and plates, scraped clean, to the cook when two riders were seen approaching. Their mounts were well fed and cared for, but the men looked weary and half-starved. One was attired in filthy, ragged pants and a Stetson which, though much the worse for hard usage, had probably cost some cowboy a month's wages. Into the waistband of his trousers was stuck a six-shooter. At first glance, his companion appeared to be wearing only a long-tailed shirt. On closer scrutiny, however, a breech-clout could be discerned underneath. Having tied their horses and placed their guns on the ground near the wagon, they walked toward the men, smiling broadly. With an extended, upturned hand, they gave their customary greeting of "How"; then, without the formality of an invitation, they hastily grabbed plates from the chuck box and helped themselves to food from Boney's pots and pans.

Their hunger appeased, they looked contentedly around. On noticing the coffee pot, one of them pointed to it and said, "Squaw sick all the time. Need pot bad."

At the same time, the other Indian was repeating over and over, as if reciting lines of poetry, one sentence, "Me got no oxie. Me got no oxie."

At this point, Red's temper flared, and he shouted at them, "By God, you'll get no oxie from this outfit; so get the hell out of here. You two, alone, could eat us out of grub in twenty-four hours."

The Indians failed to understand his words, but there was no mistaking his tone and gestures. Without further ado, they walked to their horses, picked up their guns, mounted, and rode away.

As they galloped off, Boney, who had been one of the buffalo hunters in the Adobe Walls fight, spoke up. "That's no way to get along in Indian country, and you know it. Make 'em mad enough, and they'll stampede your herd or run the whole *remuda* off."

Contrary to expectations, neither of the two Indians came to the camp the next day. However, on several occasions, small groups of Indians were seen riding in a wide circle around the wagon and horses, hollering and gesticulating as they went.

"What do you think they are after?" William asked.

Red answered, "No one ever knows exactly what an Indian wants or will do, but they look like young bucks to me, and if they are, they are trying to get us to race with them."

"Then, why doesn't one of the cowboys race? Many of them have fine ponies."

"That's true. But when the Indians race, they want something good put up like a saddle or even a horse, and most of the boys don't care to take that chance. Indians don't care. They can ride bareback as well as with a saddle, and, if they lose their horse, they'll simply steal another one."

William was crawling into his bedroll when Red called to him to get up. "I don't believe those ornery Indians will be back, but we might as well play safe and stand guard on the horses."

One of the boys raised his head long enough to say, "If you're standing guard, take that paint of mine. His eyes are as good as a cat's. He can see better in the dark than in the daylight. Besides, he's sure-footed, and there are plenty of prairie dog holes around. You'll be much safer with him under you if you have to make a run for it."

So, doubly pleased at Red's giving him a man's job to do and at having a generous friend who was willing to share his horse, William unstaked the paint pony, leaving Tex, as was his custom, to graze a little away from the other horses, near the place where he and Birl had made their beds.

When there were cattle to be herded, the men took turns, but only one cowboy ordinarily was required to watch the horses. There were twelve riding men with the wagon, and each man had, at the least, six ponies. Besides these, there were the broncs that were not yet completely broken, making a total of eighty or more. The regular night-hawk for the outfit was an oldish man, named Sam. He knew exactly how to keep those horses bunched loosely enough for grazing, but close enough together so he would have his eye on them all the time. He always rode the same horse. His instructions to William were to ride occasionally around his half; otherwise, to sit and watch.

Sam was an old hand at the job and was not only trained to stay awake, but to snatch a few winks at every opportunity that presented itself. Since the general work was still light, he had nothing to do during the day but sleep. William, on the other hand, was young and growing. He was up with the cook each morning by three-thirty or four. By sundown he was more than ready to collapse into his bedroll, to lie without waking till night was ended. The first few hours of his vigil passed without too much difficulty, but by midnight his need for sleep became overpowering. In spite of his efforts, he found himself, time and again, awaking with a start at some movement of his mount. During one of these lapses, he was suddenly startled into consciousness by the familiar neigh of a horse, followed by galloping hooves. To his embarrassment, he found himself not where he belonged, but in among the grazing horses where his pony had wandered without his knowledge.

As he rode hurriedly out, Birl shouted, "That way, over the little rise. He took Tex."

By that time, Sam was already in pursuit of the thief, with William as close as he could manage on Sam's heels. It was useless. Because of the darkness of the night, it was difficult to keep a distant and moving object in view. Before long they had lost sight of Tex and the Indian as they sped in the direction the wagon would take on the following day.

Red, although mollified, if not downright pleased, by the fact that only William's Tex had been stolen, did not miss the chance to give him one of his caustic tongue-lashings. It was not any better when William finally lay down to sleep; he continued the lashing himself. He had not only failed in his first real cowboy job, but he had lost his most enduring Panhandle friend. Question followed question in his mind. Was there any chance of recovering Tex? If not, would the Indian mistreat his horse on discovering that he had not done well by himself in the theft and had ended up with a worn-out cow pony on his hands?

During the rounding next morning, Tex was found with a badly broken leg, still lying where he had fallen after stumbling into a prairie dog hole. A shot through the head ended his misery. Although sad over his loss, William was quick to see that if he were to be of general use during the weeks to come, Red would be forced to give him a mount.

The next two days were uneventful although the wagon was nearing Comanche territory. The drought had driven the buffalo to the north, making hunting parties less common than they would have been ordinarily. As the outfit turned westward and up toward the Canadian, a Comanche band from Fort Sill discovered them. All day they hovered around, begging for a beef.

"Wohaw, oxie," they continued to call out. That was all that would satisfy them. Wishing to avoid a repetition of the raid, Red finally agreed to their pleas. Several mavericks had been picked up that morning. A good calf was roped for the leader of the party. Two of the younger men drove it off a short distance to slaughter it. At their signal the others rushed over to join them in a feast upon the still hot and bloody carcass.

"Get the hell out of here while they are satisfied," Red shouted.

As the wagon drove by, William saw a squaw and a dog, both, eating ravenously from the opposite ends of the same entrail.

For the next few days, as a punishment for his carelessness, Red refused to give him any task that required the use of a horse. William felt embarrassed and guilty at first, but, with each succeeding day, the mood was more than dispelled by his joy at being out on the plains, being with the horses and cattle and with the cowboys. He never tired of Boney's tales of his life as a buffalo hunter or of the fight at Adobe Walls. Every morning he scanned the land around him as if he had never seen it before or had recently returned home after a long absence. He enjoyed watching the horses as they grazed or the herd as it moved steadily along. It amused him to see the long body, half of which was tail, the powerful legs, and the crested head of the road-runner as it spread its wings to run with amazing speed in front of the wagon. He laughed whenever he saw a flock of loathsome and yet useful cowbirds arise from the ground to perch boldly in a body on a cow's back, there to feast on the parasites that resided in her hide. It was like discovering a treasure to see the two lavender and brown speckled eggs of the whippoorwill, lying in a depression on the prairie.

Their route ran for a short distance along the Washita. The country was beautiful. The river was not deep, but spread out wide with numerous draws leading into it. Whenever camp was made near the water, William went for a swim. It was a sport that he enjoyed but had to pursue alone, for no one else in the outfit had ever considered going into the water. Water was too highly prized a commodity to be wasted on pleasurable pursuits. When night came, he loved lying on the prairie watching the stars while the men gambled away their wages by the light of a lantern hung under the chuck box. He would not have changed lots with any other boy in the world, he told himself. All he wanted was to work the way the men worked.

CHAPTER XVII

The rounding in the Territory required only ten days. By the second night after the encounter with the Indians, Red's outfit, which was the southern division, crossed over the Canadian at a relatively shallow place to make camp at the designated rendezvous location on the north side. They would cross back into Texas late in the afternoon of the following day. The wagons from the north were already assembled. It was a riotous and relaxing night with much conversation and loud laughter and drinking, a last celebration before the start of the big roundup.

By midnight the two division bosses had planned the work in such detail that each would know the exact position of the other at all times. The northern division would do all the rounding on that side of the river; the southern division on the south. At stated intervals the herds belonging to the other division would be forced across to that side. Except for this necessary interchange of cattle, there would be no contact between the two until Adobe Walls, many miles away, was reached.

There were six separate outfits in each division. Although the boss of each outfit managed his men to a certain extent, one man had the final authority. It was Red who was given the job of running the pool to the south. His word was complete law, like that of the captain of a ship. Refusal to obey meant instant dismissal. It was only years later that William fully understood the loyalty and respect that a man with Red's qualities commanded from others, a man who was sadistically cruel and completely lacking in those sensibilities so highly regarded in a more sophisticated society. William was not yet experienced enough to realize that fearlessness, rugged strength, self-confidence, and complete disregard for personal comfort, together with a certain amount of experience, were necessary for leadership on the plains. During the weeks that followed, only one man wholeheartedly disliked Red. That man was Dave Lyle, the gunfighter. And only one hand dared to defy the boss, and that hand was William.

Between the big roundup starting point in the Territory and Adobe Walls there were numerous creeks, all tributaries of the

Canadian. Each night camp was made at a suitable place between the river and the headwaters of one of these creeks. Every morning the men rode out to round a radius of about fifteen miles, each one attached to a group of three, under the leadership of a boss selected by Red on the previous evening. Having formed a complete circle, they slowly converged, gathering the cattle as they went. There was only one roundup a day. This started around four o'clock in the morning. By noon the rounding was finished, and the cattle from the many groups were thrown together into one herd. From the beginning, it was usual for William to be given the job of holding the day herd. If it were located beyond Red's watchful eyes, he often let a cow or calf slip out in order to give himself the practice of chasing and roping the runaway. Branding was done after dinner. The days were long. The work was hard, and every man was needed.

When it came time to cross the first herd to the other side of the river, William was chosen as one of the hands to "lead out" because he was the only swimmer in the outfit. The horse that Red assigned him for this task was an excellent cow pony in all respects but one: he was mean. He never failed, upon being mounted, to throw his rider, not once but often twice, as if it were his only means of saying good morning. William took the falls stoically, picked himself up, and remounted as if they had not occurred. From that day, because of Red's need of him, he worked steadily along with the men, rounding, branding, doing anything that came along, except roping and cutting out cattle. Still he was assigned no mount of his own, and the majority of the horses left in the *remuda* were either not fully broken broncs or ponies no one, for some reason or other, wanted to ride. It clearly gave Red pleasure to put the young cowboy on the meanest horse he could find. Determined not to be fired, day after day, William picked himself up, remounted, and rode away without a word of complaint. In the beginning, he knew only one thing—that by any means possible, he must attempt to remain in the saddle.

As the days turned into weeks, William's feeling for horses and the trial-and-error method he used began to pay dividends. Gradually, without consciousness on his part, he came to recognize the kind of animal the horse was and the best way to bend the horse to his will. But what helped most was his general love of animals. His horse was his working partner, his friend. He had no desire to break the spirit of the horse or to prove which of the two was master. All he strove to do was to establish between them a relationship that would be pleasant for both.

He tried not to overlook a thing. His ambition, at the time, was to become a bronc buster, not only because the buster was considered a top hand, but because he received a five-dollar bonus for every horse he broke. He began to watch Fred at work and to note the reaction of the horse to the man whose one idea was to show who was boss. From the time Fred mounted, it was an open contest, with Fred raking the animal's sides with his spurs and madly twirling his rope to add to the bronc's terror. William felt that this was not the method by which to achieve the best results. With his sympathy on the side of the dumb brute, he often wished silently for the bronc buster to be thrown; and if the contest were unusually severe, he always tried afterward to get as near as possible to the horse to talk to him in a quiet voice. He himself never mounted, at the start of the day, without first patting and saying a few words to the partner upon which depended much of his own success or failure during the hours to follow. And he could not wait for the day to come when he could stay on a bronc as well as Fred.

It was not long after William began working with the men that Red made his first conciliatory remark.

"I'll have to say one thing for you, kid. You are a game little cuss. There's an outlaw over there among the broncs. If you can break him, he's yours; also that pony that throws you every morning. Then you'll have a string. It may be a short string, but it will be one of your own anyway."

William was jubilant. Praise from Red, even grudging praise, seemed to him the highest accolade one could get.

The pony in question was a magnificent-looking animal, compactly built, with beautiful balance and harmony of movement. He had small, restless ears, bright, lively eyes, a long neck, and fine black hair that grew in abundance. He was a real beauty, but he jumped wildly at any attempt to place anything around his neck. Turning to a nearby cowboy, William said, "I'll have to have some help in catching him. If you will rope and bring him in, I'll saddle up and get on while you hold him."

As the cowboy prepared to swing his rope, he said, "Every horse should have a name. What are you going to call this one?" William replied, "I don't have time to think of that now. Maybe I will just call him my pony."

After considerable effort, the bronc was made ready, and William climbed on. With his knees pressed in tight, he took a firm grip on the reins. Keep that head up, if you can, he thought. Once the rope was off the pony's neck, the pony went wild. Up into the air, back arched, and down again on stiff forelegs, with the jolt that on occasion had thrown some of the best riders. William managed to stay on. Up again, down again, time after time. Suddenly changing tactics, the pony reared straight up, as if preparing to fall backwards on his rider. William refused to jump off. The pony pawed the earth and tossed his head frantically. All at once he quieted down and stood for a moment. Then, in one final effort, he bolted. Away they raced, with the bodies of boy and pony moving in perfect unison. Across the plain and out of sight.

The watching cowboy said, "God, look at that boy ride."[1]

Half an hour later, when William came loping back in the easy manner so characteristic of the cowboy, he was filled with pride on hearing the cowboy say to Red, "Boss, looks like the outfit's got a new bronc buster."

Thus William's days passed happily and busily. As the work progressed, he was called on to do more and more until suddenly, before he knew it, he found himself to be an integrated part of the whole. Riding was becoming almost second nature to him. Each day was spent largely in the saddle, either galloping after a recalcitrant cow or moving from place to place in a slow jog.

As the roundups continued, the work increased for everyone. It

---

[1] William learned to stay on any kind of horse but lacked the grace to make him what is called a "good" rider. His forte lay in his ability to understand horses. As a result, he became an excellent bronc buster.

was not too long before the herd reached a size that required its being guarded constantly at night. The time assigned each cowboy remained his for the duration of the trip. William was one of the shift that stood guard from eleven-thirty to one-thirty, which meant that every night's rest was broken squarely in the middle. Of everything he had to do this was the most difficult, but pride and the memory of his failure on his first attempt gave him added determination. He used various methods to keep awake. On the occasions when none of the others proved efficacious and his lids seemed determined to close, as a last resort he rubbed tobacco juice into his eyes. In general, by the time the stinging sensation had ceased, his attack of drowsiness was over. After a while, like the other men, he learned to snatch a few moments whenever possible, often in the saddle at the side of the herd. He knew instinctively when his watch was ended; he also knew when it began and, long before the drive was nearing its conclusion, he was beginning to wake up at eleven o'clock without being called.

Red continued to give William the job of leading out when a herd was to be delivered across the river. In that part of the country, the Canadian, except after heavy rains, was mostly a wide sand bed, through the center of which flowed a small stream. Even in the few places where the stream deepened to three or four feet, it was still not more than twenty feet wide, with low, sloping banks where plums and grapes grew in abundance and tall cottonwoods offered welcome shade. In spite of its harmless appearance, it was "quickie"—hazardous because of quicksand—and filled with sand bars and holes, both of which were as dangerous to the men as to the horses.

One afternoon before Adobe Walls was reached, William started across with a bunch of cattle. Because the river appeared to be shallow and without danger, he did not provide himself with a gentle horse but waded in on Buck, the outlaw pony, one of the two horses given him by Red. Although Buck had become tractable enough to allow himself to be saddled, he still continued to throw his rider now and then. A few feet out, the water suddenly deepened. As it rose toward Buck's flanks, he became fractious. In throwing his hind legs about, one of them went off into a hole. He floundered for a few minutes, then, after tiring, ceased struggling, in spite of William's continued efforts to keep him moving. He sank quickly, and immediately swirling water was all around William and his entangled horse. Meanwhile, the two boys who had come to the rescue discovered that the hole was at the side of a sand bar that ran the width of the stream. They put their horses ashore and returned to the spot on foot. Carefully, so as not to sink into the hole themselves, they took positions on the far side of the horse. Having first tramped down with their feet a solid place on the side opposite the bar, they rapidly churned the water and sand around first one, then the other of Buck's hind legs, until both were released sufficiently for him to be pulled to the bank. No real injury had come to the pony. Nevertheless, he was frantic. William worked with him for days but was never able to ride him again.

Finding himself once more in the awkward position of not having a mount of his own, William turned his attention toward the broncs. He had not had sufficient time to spend on the other pony, which as yet was unfit for steady work. Having gotten Red's permission, William chose for his third attempt at bronc busting a little paint that appeared to have a gentler nature than the others he had worked with. He roped and saddled him, talking all the while, then climbed on. As usual, down came the front feet, up went the back, out went the hind legs, and they were off. William was thrown, then thrown again, and again and again he remounted. He had almost reached the point of admitting defeat when the pony bucked once more, then suddenly stopped short and broke into a run. Round and round he raced until he and William were both worn down.

When they returned to camp, Fred, who had been watching with amusement, grabbed the paint's bridle and said, "Why don't you call it a day? I have an idea this little horse ain't goin' to give you a bit more trouble. You didn't know it, but you've been working with the mean ones. Most broncs only buck a few times, and then are all through."

William accepted his advice and unsaddled. When he approached the little paint the next morning, it stood quietly as he bridled it, saddled it, mounted, and rode off. From that day on it was as good a cow pony as any pony in the *remuda*.

A few days later the wagons reached Adobe Walls, the 1874 scene of the bloody battle between the buffalo hunters and the warring Comanches under the famous half-breed Comanche leader, Quanah Parker, their last chief and the son of a captive white girl and Chief Peta Nocona to whom she was married. It was the first meeting of the two divisions. A celebration was in order. Once again there was much drinking, singing, and dancing without girls. William watched the festivities for a while, then wandered off to inspect the site where the battle of Adobe Walls had been fought. There was nothing left of the picket and sod structures that had formed the stockade, but through Boney's many descriptions William was able to form a mental picture of the saloon, the blacksmith shop, and the store inside which the buffalo hunters prepared to meet the Comanche attack. It was much more exciting than watching cowboys drink and dance to the tune of a fiddle. Although the gaiety continued till morning, it did not interfere with his sleep.

By noon of the next day, everyone was sober and ready to go to work. As soon as the interchange of cattle had been made, the divisions parted, each to continue rounding on its side of the river until the next meeting place out of Tascosa was reached. The addition of the cattle from across the river increased the herd to a size too unwieldy to handle. In order to diminish the number, Red decided to separate the Heart, Spade, R. O., and Half Circle K cattle from the others for immediate return to their home ranges. As far as possible, an attempt was made never to allow the pool herd to exceed twenty-five hundred. To William's pleased surprise, he was ordered by Red to assist old man Cummins of the Heart Ranch in driving the cattle back as far as Carroll Creek.

They left at dawn the following morning. During the preceding days there had been little time for William to follow up his first hard ride on the pony without a name, and, unfortunately, the pony appeared to be the kind of bronc that had to be rebroken every time he was ridden. By keeping a close watch on Fred's technique, William had noticed that on one or two occasions Fred had ridden around with the bronc he was trying to break tied to the saddle horn of his mount. As a last measure, William decided to try that with the pony. If the long trip to the Heart pasture and back had no taming effect, he would be forced to tell Red that he, like the several others who had attempted it, was not able to break the pony. When the herd moved out, he was riding the good, steady, little paint. The stubborn and fractious pony, much against his will, followed along at the end of a short rope.

It was William's first experience in real trail driving, although the pool herd had to be moved each day. Like previous experiences, this one proved to be hard. There were fifteen hundred cattle with only the man and the boy to handle them, which meant they not only stayed in the saddle all day, but had to take turns holding the herd through the night. Their only food consisted of the bacon and biscuit they carried in their bedrolls and innumerable cups of campfire coffee.

Each day they followed the same routine, with a distance of fifteen or more miles covered, according to the availability of water. The weaker steers and the few cows and calves were placed at the back of the herd. Cummins rode ahead to lead the way; William followed in the very rear, to make certain no animal strayed off far enough to be lost. Because it is the habit of cattle to wander aimlessly for a short length of time before settling down to graze, Cummins pushed them out at the first sign of light. By the time morning had fully arrived, he allowed them to graze and drink again, while he and William made coffee and ate their meager breakfast; then they started the herd moving again. If given an opportunity to graze well and drink just before sundown, the animals would bed down peacefully. Because no storms came up and there was no loud and unexpected noise, they gave little trouble through the nights. The drive was finished without mishap, and the cattle were turned loose on the lush grasses of Carroll Creek. It was a real temptation, after days of limited food, to go home for one good meal, but William resisted the urge. After a few hours' rest, he and the old man were on their way back to the Canadian.

Since every hour of the ride down had been filled with some special duty, William had found little time to devote to the pony. He had managed to get a saddle on him on the morning of the last day before reaching Carroll Creek. As the time came to saddle up for the return trip, Cummins noticed William was saddling the unruly bronc, instead of the reliable paint.

"Are you trying to get yourself killed?" Cummins said. "That's a mean critter and would give anybody trouble, 'specially a feller that don't wear boots. The first thing you know, one of your feet'll slip through that stirrup and you'll be dragged till you're dead."

"I know it could happen, but I don't think it will. I watched him all day yesterday with that saddle, and I've decided he bucks when the cinch belt is too tight on his belly. That makes him mad. Anyway, I'm going to loosen it up just a little. Then you're going to tie my feet together under him. Come on, help me. I can't get on him unless you do."

With the aid of a cottonwood to which the pony was tied, they managed to bridle and saddle him. As soon as William's feet were made fast, Cummins loosened the rope and let the bronc go, with the encouraging remark that it all looked like suicide to him.

Pony went up into the air only once, then, instead of bucking again, started to run. He raced over the plains like something mad, with William giving him his head, but holding on tight with his knees. He made no effort to stop Pony or guide him, except for an occasional pull on one rein to keep him running in a circle instead of away from camp. After a while Pony wore himself out. By the time they returned to camp, he was giving no more trouble. William rode him all that day and every succeeding day of the return trip.

The ride back north was a pleasant respite from duty, practically a vacation. Although William never felt lonely when alone on the prairie, he still suffered a little from the feeling that he was not yet an accepted member of the outfit; but Cummins was treating him like an equal, as simply another man doing his job. William was secretly delighted and felt more and more grateful to the Heart cowboy as they rode along.

Like the majority of elderly people, the old man was full of talk.

Before the trip was ended, William had heard all there was to relate about buffalo hunting, trail driving, and the various outfits with which Cummins had worked. There was one bit of gossip toward the end that struck too close to home for comfort. Cummins was discussing the Heart outfit to which he belonged.

"You oughta come eat with our wagon sometime. We git things nobody ever heard of givin' to a cowboy. The company's goin' broke anyway, so it don't make no never-mind what they throw away on feedin' the boys. Nobody'll ever know the difference. That preacher Carhart had some funny ideas for a Methody soul-saver. He'd talk to you about not breaking the Ten Commandments on Sunday, and, on Monday, would tell a good old man like Tabor that this was the finest farm land anywhere around. I hear that some count from one o' them furrin' places is comin' over soon to take it all over. Carhart's already quit cow-punchin' and gone back to his old business, preachin'. Anyway, we'll find out when we git back to town." He was quiet for a few minutes, then said, "I heard that uncle of yours is too big for his britches. What about it?"

William had never felt drawn to his uncle, and he had often heard doubts expressed over Bill's competence as a cattleman. However, he had a suspicion that Cummins was talking chiefly to draw him out. Because of his loyalty to the family in general, he left the question unanswered. Nevertheless, the implications in Cummins' gossip worried him. If a huge company like the Quarter Circle Heart, with capable stockmen like Al McKinney and Judge Murdock in charge, was in trouble, what chance was there for the Half Circle K, whose manager was never around?

They rode back into camp toward sundown; William, with a little tingle of pride, was still mounted on Pony, who had become almost as gentle as the paint. They had been gone just a week. The next morning Cummins and he were riding hard in the big roundup again.

CHAPTER XVIII

Beyond Adobe Walls, the Canadian River valley gradually disappeared. As it did, the river deepened and narrowed, and its waters became icy cold. In only a few places were there even slightly sloping banks. Instead, the plains extended directly to the edge of the steep cliffs, which rose straight up from the river like a wall on either side. For several days, it was unbearably hot and sultry, with thunderheads and heat lightning presaging the storm that often climaxed that kind of weather.

"I hope," grumbled Red, "that all hell don't break loose and stampede these cattle before we get that northern bunch across the river. We could lose many a head on these high banks."

When the storm came, however, its fury was centered many miles away, near the headwaters of the Canadian, and the steady rain, which followed as an aftermath, neither disturbed the cattle nor retarded Red's progress in reaching a suitable crossing place. They found one late the following day. By then the river had risen steadily, reaching a level that would enable the men to crowd the cattle on this side into the water. On the opposite, not too far distant, bank was an opening between the cliffs, providing the slope necessary to get the cattle out of the water and onto the land.

Camp was made with the plan to cross the herd in the morning when they would not be forced to face the sun. The rain let up about midnight. Long before dawn, while the men were still at breakfast, Red was shouting, "Whoop'em up, boys. She's rising every minute, so don't waste any time. Strip down, Billy, and get ready to lead'em out."

Even though unable to swim, the men did not question the order. They were so familiar with such crossings they did not even stop to consider the hazards involved. As usual, William was expected to ride out and into the river ahead of the herd. At the rear were the "drags" whose job it was to keep the cattle moving so briskly that on reaching the cliffs their own momentum would force them into the water, which otherwise they would have balked at entering. Once in, the cattle would instinctively swim to shore.

As the others rode back to start the herd moving, William saddled, shed down to his undergarments, mounted, and started toward the edge of the cliff. Once there, he saw a fairly alarming spectacle. The usually calm waters were threshing and foaming. Tossing about on the high waves were logs and tree trunks, even an occasional boulder, which had been picked up in the stream's forward rush. He was sure enough of his own skill in the water to have no fear of the water itself, but he saw at a glance the dangers that lurked in a bad undertow if there was one. He was certain, also, that a strong and intelligent horse like Pony could successfully combat the current, but the probability of any cowboy's remaining in the saddle was slight, and, once off, he would not get any distance before he was either sucked under or hit by a heavy piece of debris that would kill him instantly or render him helpless. It was not logical to risk the life of one or more men in order to get a bunch of cattle to the other side on a certain day.

When he got to Red, the herd was already moving. There was no time to explain anything; all the same, William felt it his duty to warn Red.

"Neither man nor animal could make it across that river the way it is now; and, I, for one, have no intention of trying to," he shouted.

To think one of his hands would dare to question an order made Red furious. With a shake of the fist he hollered back, "Not leading out? Yes, you are or you're fired. Around here, I'm the one who makes the decisions. Have you forgotten that?"

William was aware of that, and he liked his job, but he liked life more. Red, apparently, was adamant. There was nothing further he could do but turn his horse in the direction of camp, go back, pick up his bedroll, and start at once on the long ride back to Clarendon.

Behind him, Red was hollering in his rage, "All right, then, I'm no yellow-bellied coward of a tenderfoot. I'll just lead out myself. Follow me, boys!" And, with a touch of his spurs, he started at full gallop toward the river.

William, realizing that Red could not swim, turned to see the outcome of such foolhardiness. It was Red's good fortune that he was on his favorite mount, a horse that was not only spirited but also so gentle that it followed its master around like a dog; nonetheless, on reaching the water, the usually docile animal refused to take the plunge. Red, with mounting fury, turned and rode back for fifty yards, then wheeled and drove the horse at a savage gallop to the edge of the bank and into the turbulent Canadian. Both horse and Red sank instantly out of sight. They did not reappear for what seemed an eternity to William, Art Sherrod, and Fred Patchin, as they leaned forward to watch. When rider and pony finally came to the surface, they were already some distance down the stream, but fairly close to the bank. Red was hanging on to the pony's tail. It was quite clear that, in falling, the horse turned over on one side, unseating Red. Somehow, Red had managed to slip off over the rump and catch hold of the tail.

Art and Fred rode along the river's edge, their lariats in readiness to catch the pony's neck the moment it was far enough above the water. They finally managed it. Red was back on the bank with the men, who were wondering, now that they had time, how Red had kept from being pawed to death by the frenzied pony's hooves and how he had managed to keep his head above the raging water.

Although half-drowned, coughing, too weak to stand, and blood-bespattered from a big gash in his head, Red was his old undaunted self. When William started toward the camp again to pack his paraphernalia, he was pulled up short by Red's hoarse shout.

"What the hell do you think you're doin' now?"

"I'm getting ready to go home."

"Take that God-damn bedroll off and put it in the wagon where it belongs. There's too much work to be done to waste time on your foolishness."

It was all Red ever said. No word of explanation, no admission that he might have been in the wrong; yet William understood that behind the oath and the hoarse command it was all there, and this time he happily obeyed. It was his initiation into manhood, into the tribe, the formal acceptance of him as one of their own by these rough men. There was no longer any question, he knew, in the minds of any one of them as to whether or not he was a cowboy and a full-fledged member of the Half Circle K outfit.

CHAPTER XIX

A few days later the outfit reached Tascosa. Camp was made where the stream broke out from the hills, among the many *atascosas*—or boggy islets—that gave the settlement its Spanish name. The wagon stood in the center of a cottonwood grove. Willows bordered the creeks, and beaver dams cluttered their waters. Wild turkeys roosted by the hundreds in the distant trees. It was a welcome change from the barren country that bordered much of the Texas Canadian.

Since the two divisions were to separate permanently while there, time was needed to divide the cattle. Furthermore, this was the obvious place to give the boys a few days of relaxation and respite from work. Before the conclusion of supper, two local Mexicans rode up with an invitation to a dance at which the cowboys would supply the music. Boney did a jig, and hats flew into the air as they yelled their approval.

It was the beginning of a rough and bawdy celebration, for Tascosa was in perfect accord with the hardness of the region that surrounded it. Its population, unlike the church-going nucleus that gave Clarendon its tone, was a colorful aggregation of humanity, so foreign to anything William had ever before seen that it appeared almost unreal, more like a scene from fiction. On the streets were cowboys with six-shooters, gamblers, desperadoes, dance-hall girls, and an occasional señorita in a mantilla, or a priest in cassock and biretta. At the edge of town was a district known as Hog-town. In the large adobe building where most of the neighborhood's activities were centered was a long room that extended all the way across the front. At one end was the bar. A door at the back led into a passageway that gave access to several small rooms. The dance was held in the front room.

Most of the girls were Mexicans who spoke almost no English. The cowboys spoke no Spanish. The language barrier apparently had no effect on the gaiety of the evening. By midnight, the party had turned into a drunken fracas, with one of the Spur men brandishing his gun in a threatening manner. At any unexpected incident the revel could become a tragedy.

To the embarrassment of William and the amusement of the cowboys, one of the girls left her partner to approach him. Taking his hand, she said, "Leetle Americano, will you danz wis me?"

His pleasure on seeing a girl of his own age and his desire to take part in the fun overcame his shyness and his fear that he might be laughed at. He got slowly to his feet and was grateful to his pretty little black-eyed partner for seizing his hand, placing his arm around her waist, and making him move out among the dancers. As he struggled to move as gracefully as she among the jostling couples, he found that holding the pretty Mexican girl in his arms was a most pleasing sensation, one that made him feel like a man. When the music stopped, he led her to the wall where some older Mexican women stood watching and with mumbled thanks beat a hasty retreat.

He walked slowly back to camp, his eyes drawn in the moonlit night to the myraids of stars and the moon that seemed to be laughing at him. His mingled excitement and disappointment over the little Mexican girl haunted him. Once in his bedroll, however, it was only a few minutes before he was asleep—and dreaming, first, that he owned a whole string of broncs like Pony, and later, that he was dancing and dancing with a blonde girl, the fragrance of whose cool skin and golden hair he breathed in with delight.

CHAPTER XX

Three days later the divisions parted, Red's wagons following a course to the southeast. On leaving the Canadian and its tributaries, they entered one of the world's largest plains. The face of the landscape was not the same as that of the lake country. For miles on every side there was nothing but a boundless tableland of grass[1] moving in slow undulations with the wind. Not a creek, not an arroyo, not a tree broke the monotony of the expanse. Only an occasional small cloud appeared, to float away as quickly as it came. The sun beat down mercilessly. Heat waves shimmered up from the earth in glistening succession. A burning wind blew throughout the day without cessation. It was an isolated world all its own.

Farther to the south, the Palo Duro and the Tierra Blanca creeks cut across in different directions to flow down the plain's gentle slope to their point of juncture in the Palo Duro Canyon where they became the Prairie Dog Fork of Red River. It was Red's plan to start rounding near the headwaters of the Palo Duro, to follow the creek almost to the canyon, then to move back westward along the Tierra Blanca, all the way into New Mexico.

The route to be traveled crossed and recrossed the vast free grass area used by all the cattlemen. It was an expanse fifteen miles wide and fifty miles long, bounded on the east by the T Anchor, and on the west by three million acres of the XIT, the most unpopular outfit in the Panhandle. The T Anchor was a part of the pool, but not the XIT, whose owners and operators were Eastern financiers who had no intention either of becoming Texans or of adopting the customs of the region. The lax business methods of the majority of the cattlemen were openly frowned upon by the XIT financiers. As a result, they were heartily disliked both by cowboys and ranchmen, and the XIT never participated in the general roundup. It was amusing to William to watch the pleasure with which Red sighted an XIT calf and the dispatch with which he had it slaughtered. On no other part of the drive did the men enjoy the luxury of so much beef.

The Palo Duro headwaters rose within the XIT pasture, not too far from the ranch's boundary line, and the pasture below the Palo Duro, watered by the Tierra Blanca, was still unfenced, and for all practical purposes free grass range. Camp was made on the first night several miles to the east of the XIT boundary. The very first day, while he was rounding with Art Sherrod, William saw a bunch

---

[1] Except for the previous winter of 1885–1886, the Panhandle had been in a long rainy cycle. With abundant moisture, grama thrived and sometimes reached a height of eighteen inches.

of plains antelope. There were not too many of them since, as Art told him, it was characteristic of antelope to break away from the big herd in the spring to form smaller bunches. They were a pretty sight, with their tall horns pointing upward and their small and graceful bodies, so like the landscape in color that a single one lying on the earth might easily have been overlooked. William started at once to ride nearer in order to examine them more closely, but the antelope, shy like all plains animals, fled as soon as the first beat of his horse's hooves reached their ears. Only one, more intrepid than the others, stopped to inquire into the nature of the approaching object.

"They sure make fine eating," Art said. "It would be a welcome change from beef. But you'll never get one. Jackrabbits and antelope can outrun any horse."

In spite of Art's discouragement, William readied his gun. It was useless. Before he was in shooting range, the animal raced off to join his companions.

"There is one way that works. At least, Fred Patchin says it works, and he bagged more of 'em than anyone I know. He swears that all he does is to get as close to 'em as they'll let him. Then he lies down so his body will be out of sight, and, with a red rag tied to one foot, he raises his leg in the air and waves it back and forth. They're as curious as a woman, he says, and sooner or later one of 'em will have to find out what's goin' on and come close enough to be shot at."

William took it all in. People on the plains had such unusual ways of doing things he was not certain whether Art was serious or was teasing him. Anyway, he was going to try it. As soon as he was through with the days' work, he made up his mind that he was going to return to the spot where he had seen the antelope—with a gun, of course, but with a red kerchief, too, just in case there was something to Art's tale. As soon as he and Art got the herd they were rounding back to camp, he would borrow a gun and slip away without notice, if possible, so as not to be laughed at on his return if his efforts failed.

However, when he asked Red for the gun, he was overheard by a cowboy who, strangely enough, was one of the few members of the outfit with whom William was not already on the friendliest of terms. After much insistence on the cowboy's part, William told him what he was planning to do. Long after the incident with its tragic end was over, William was still wondering whether the cowboy accompanied him simply to be a witness to a good joke or because he was so bored he was ready to do anything.

They located the antelope, still grazing, not far from camp. Before getting close enough to frighten them, William and the cowboy staked their horses, and, after walking a distance away, lay down. Once in position, William raised the leg with the handkerchief tied to it and began to move it slowly back and forth. He kept this up for what seemed to him an interminable length of time, during which the cowboy said nothing.

Finally, William got up in disgust. He said, careful to keep his voice low, "I should have known Art was trying to play a joke on me. Come on. Let's try once more to get close enough for a shot. If the antelope run, we'll have to quit and give up for today. We'll try again some other time."

Finding their luck with the gun no better than that with the handkerchief, they turned back to camp. "We'll have to hurry," William said, "or we will be late for supper and Boney will be mad at me, not you."

They were riding briskly along when something neither had noticed in the way ahead made the cowboy's horse shy. The bronc's violent jump to one side caused the saddle to slip in the opposite direction, in a manner that left the rider hanging far over the side, with one foot out of the stirrup and dangling almost to the ground. Almost instantly there was an ominous rattle and a loud "God damn," and William knew that the thing on the ground was a snake and that the snake had struck.

After catching the startled horse not far from the accident, William stopped only long enough to glance hurriedly at the enemy on the ground. By now he was familiar with rattlers. This one was not only larger but had unusual markings. Also, instead of slithering away, it was still coiled for action, its fierce head high in the air and its tail rattling vigorously. Even though the reptile had a striking reach of two thirds its length, it was not personal fear that stopped William from shooting him, but his fear for the life of the groaning cowboy.

By the time they rode in, the injured man was in a heavy sweat and had commenced vomiting.

"Pour the whiskey down him, while I burn the filth off this knife," Boney shouted, at the same time holding the blade of his pocket knife into the blaze of his supper fire. "After that, go get some mud from the creek. That's all a horse ever does—just stands in the mud—and I've yet to see one die from snake bite."

As soon as the liquor had taken effect, the cook cut a deep and wide wound, in an attempt to bleed and suck out the poison. None of his efforts seemed to abate its spread. The wound no longer bled but oozed an ugly, yellow pus while the sick man's entire body slowly distended. His fever rose; his heartbeat weakened, and his breath came with difficulty. He died as dawn broke over the plains.

They buried him the same morning. The grave was shallow so they piled as many rocks as they could find on top. When they were finished, they harnessed the horses to the wagon, saddled up, and started to ride off across the plain.

Something still remained to be done. Fred agreed, and they rode back to find the snake. It was still there, as aggressive as ever, its long, loathsomely thick, mottled gray and brown body so like the color of the ground, it was no wonder neither William's horse nor the cowboy's had noticed it until too late. At their approach now, it coiled and rattled menacingly.

"You low son of Satan," Fred growled and with one blast from his shotgun blew its head off. When the ugly body of the rattler had quieted down from its death coilings and recoilings, they went up close to examine it.

"This fellow's over six feet long," Fred said. "Just notice them diamond squares. It's a diamondback.[2] I never seen one before. Sure is funny the way things happen, ain't it? They're as scarce as hen's

---

[2] The plains are not the habitat of the diamondback, but my husband did run across two of them.

teeth in these parts. With all this big country to choose from, the poor cowboy had to ride onto this one."

When William shuddered and turned away, Fred went on, "Don't worry; you ain't to blame. There wasn't anything anybody could do. Not even the strongest man could have lived after a bite from that big bastard."

But William was not consoled. Only this morning, just a few hours ago, the cowboy had been alive. Only yesterday afternoon he had been riding in search of antelope. For many succeeding nights, William slept fitfully. His one hope was that the cowboy loved the plains as he himself loved them and would always feel at home in his lonely resting place.

CHAPTER XXI

By the first of July the wagons were in New Mexico. The rounding on the creeks was finished. They were ready to start for home. The drive down from Tascosa had been the most grueling part of the summer's work. Many of the lakes, which during the previous long rainy cycle dotted the landscape, had disappeared. Since the drought, only the major creeks ran water. The others had turned into disappointing arroyos. Not since the storm on the Canadian had there been even a promise of rain. By midday the temperature soared to 112 degrees or more. From fourteen to sixteen hours each day the men were in the saddle, and the cowboy's untimely death not only had cast a gloom over the outfit but also had given the more superstitious the idea that it meant bad luck. It was none too soon for a holiday when they stopped to make camp on a good-sized lake near Fort Sumner, not too far from the Pecos River. It was a pleasant spot, with clumps of tall cottonwoods and marsh grasses all around the water's edge. On the opposite banks some Indians had set up their teepees in preparation for the coming celebration.

"Day after tomorrow's the Fourth," Red said. "Fort Sumner's a good place to have fun. You can find most anything you want to do in that rambling old building that used to be the army hospital. Besides, there are races all the time on the flat beyond the river. We're going to take a day or two off. The last few weeks have been kinda rough goin'. Ride into town, some of you, and find out what's on tap."

The dance at Tascosa had given William his fill of cowboy entertainment, but he was eager to have a look at Fort Sumner, the place that had once been a frontier stronghold and also the stomping ground, as Red called it, of Billy the Kid. It took only one trip, however, to show him there was little of interest in town for him. A large ramshackle frame house, a double row of adobes, and an unkempt square of grass were the only indications that an army post, with officers' club, hospital, barracks, and parade ground, had predated the town. Numerous saloons and stores, all backing up to the river, lined the main street. Along its dirty board sidewalks meandered the rowdiest crowd of riffraff he could imagine: señoritas in Mexican dress, gamblers with tall hats and checkered waistcoats, cowboys with gun in holster, much-bedecked prostitutes with painted faces and lips, confidence men, and half-naked Indians. By the door of the general store was a large sign—"Races tomorrow. Enter your horse inside."

William suddenly had an idea.

"Let's get back to the wagon," he said to the cowboy who had come into town with him. "I want to talk to Red about racing Pony."

A little to William's surprise, the foreman was not only agreeable but downright eager to be helpful.

"Good," he said, "we'll have to fill up with supplies tomorrow. While you and Boney do that, I'll enter your horse in a race or two. We won't have much time; so here's the list and tomorrow you ride in a little ahead of us and get the things together. I'll drive in with Boney."

As soon as breakfast was over the following morning, William saddled the paint and was off for town. About the middle of the morning he saw Red and Boney drive in with the rest of the outfit following close behind.

It required about half the morning to get the supplies loaded into the wagon, after which William mounted his horse and hurried to join the others at the race track. People had evidently been gathering there all morning. The slope above the river bottom, which served as grandstand, was swarming, mostly with boisterous cowboys. Red was in the midst of them, exhibiting a convivial manner very unlike his usual self. He came over to the Half Circle K group just long enough to give William instructions for the races.

"You are in the second, fourth, and eighth races. You'll get twenty-five dollars for every race you win, and fifty more if you take more of 'em than anybody else. I might even add a little something to that myself. I'd sure like to see one of the Half Circle K boys win." Then, abruptly, in a more usual voice, he added, "And see that you win."

William knew that he was a good rider and that he would have a fast horse under him. He also knew that the same thing was true of most of the other entries. Among them were several Mescalero Apaches, and there were no better horsemen anywhere on the plains; furthermore, each of them would have managed, by fair means or foul, to be in possession of a good horse.

Two things cheered him. He was light in weight, and he was determined to win. The prize money, together with his wages, would make it possible for him to do something he had been thinking about for the last few weeks. If he won, he would inquire around to see if there was a way for someone who was not yet of age to file on land. He would also be able to buy a pistol that he especially liked.

He won the first race, lost the second, and won the last. He did not come out champion. An Apache boy of his own age accomplished that, but he was more than satisfied. In one afternoon he had earned as much as a cowboy would receive for several months of work.

On his return to camp, he found the men in a state of jubilation quite unwarranted by the mere fact of his winning two races. Everyone had a handful of money. Red pressed twenty-five dollars into his hand. As he did, he laughed and said, "I sure fooled these Indians and New Mexico cowboys. I told them you were nothing but a smart alec kid, the son of one of the ranch's three owners. That you were determined to show off—that you really didn't know anything about riding a horse."

CHAPTER XXII

On leaving Fort Sumner, the wagons turned completely around to move in a straight course eastward. Midway across the plains, the Diamond F, T Anchor, and J. A. hands cut for home, leaving only three wagons in the pool. The weather continued hot. On the first day out thunder clouds appeared only to disappear within a few hours. There was an oppressive quality to the atmosphere. This continued through the next morning and afternoon. About sundown, without much warning, the sky was suddenly overcast. Not a single star shone through to break the blackness of early night.

"Looks bad," said Red. "We may be in for trouble, and this damned bedding ground is riddled with prairie dog holes. We'd better double the guard, and every man keep a horse ready so's he can ride on a moment's notice."

As the storm drew near, the cattle grew more restless. Those that were not already milling lay halfway up on their forelegs. In spite of the efforts of the boys, they continued to break from the herd in an instinctive urge to move ahead of the approaching storm. Around midnight the storm hit with all the fury of a giant's pent-up wrath. A bolt of lightning tore into the ground at the edge of the herd. At the resounding peal of thunder, which followed instantly, the cattle broke. After that, there was no holding them.

The violence of the storm lasted for a full half-hour, making the plain a scene of bedlam. Cattle ran wildly in every direction, with all the cowboys in mad pursuit. Lightning struck repeatedly, on some occasions sending a ball of fire across the ground. The air was filled with a stifling odor of sulphur, and electricity played on the horns of the animals. Added to the commotion was the deafening clatter and thud of hooves, and of shouting men. Then came the rain and then hail. By the end of the storm, the herd was scattered far and wide. Even the *remuda* had stampeded.

By the time William got back to camp with all the cattle he could find and several horses, Boney already had a huge fire going and the coffee pot on. The men were standing around the fire drying out their soaked clothes and talking about the storm. William was almost the last of them to come in.

"Where the hell have you been?" Red shouted at him. "Cattle may be our business, but on a night like this, I want to be damn sure all my men are accounted for." Then, after looking inquiringly around, he continued, "Who is missing?"

"I think it is the Mexican boy from the south," William answered, "and I'm afraid he is dead. When the big bolt came, he was riding toward me; then there was another flash, and he was nowhere around. It hit so close, I don't know why it didn't kill both my horse and me. I saw his horse stumble. The saddle must have slipped; all I know is he was turning toward the cattle. It was all so quick and dark."

One of the other cowboys had also been close to the Mexican boy when the lightning struck. Between his account and William's, the others were able to piece out what had probably happened. They were all borne down by gloom but still continued to hope that the missing man might show up. He did not come.

They found him soon after daybreak, about a quarter of a mile from the bedding ground, trampled beyond recognition. His horse was lying close to a big hole made in the ground by the lightning. They could only guess what had happened. When the horse stumbled, he had evidently been thrown. Ordinarily the steers would not have run over a man on the ground, but, as both William and the other cowboy remembered only too well, the stampeding cattle had been bunched so close together there would have been no way for them to avoid him even if they had seen him.

No one spoke for a few moments. Red turned to look William directly in the face and, in his gruffest voice, said, "When you and the Mexican failed to show up along with the others, I was sure one of you was hurt. Because of those God-damned shoes you ride in, I thought it was you." Then in an even harsher tone, he added, "If you don't learn to wear boots[1] like every other cowboy, you are not long for this world whether lightning strikes you or not."

[1] Boots are the cowboy's chief safeguard against accidents. The heel of the boot helps prevent his foot from slipping through and being caught in the stirrup.

The young stampede victim was buried as quickly as the grave could be dug, and, as though nothing had happened, the men resumed their work. Nobody talked much during the rest of the day. They went immediately to work, and there was much to do. It was three days before the horses and all the cattle were rounded and the wagons were again homeward bound. All along the way, the grass had been beaten into the ground by the hail. Hundreds of dead jackrabbits lay everywhere.

CHAPTER XXIII

Their next stop was close to the jutting tip of a ravine. The ravine was one of a series of small canyons that formed the Palo Duro. At that point, the cliffs began to dwindle and the canyon bed to spread out into prairie land. It was here that the Prairie Dog Fork, with added width, assumed the name of Red River. Since the wagons had missed the place where the Palo Duro and Tierra Blanca joined, this was William's first view of the canyon, a yawning chasm that extended for sixty miles across the plains. In places, the cliffs rose straight up for a thousand feet, with turrets of clay that gave the whole much the appearance of a mighty feudal castle. Cottonwood trees spread their shade over the waters that ran below, while the green of the many cedars softened the harshness of the scene, and the yellows, browns, and reds of foliage and sand added bits of vivid color. Numerous cave-like holes yawned in the clay cliffs, some of them extending far back into the earth. In the small ones rattlesnakes hibernated in winter and, in summer, retreated from the heat of the sun. In the larger ones, the lobos sought shelter and raised their cubs.

In the morning the wagon moved out, a "loafer"—a leisurely roaming lobo—was seen in the distance, feeding on a recent kill. As Red rode toward her to examine her prey, she trotted lazily away. The fact that the steer bore a Half Circle K brand and was still warm infuriated the foreman.

"The dirty cowards, stalking a poor dumb animal till they get close enough to cripple it, just so they can eat it alive. Stop here," he called to the others. "It may be noon before we get back. The damned old thing is a bitch, and she'll sure take the long way home to protect her young 'uns, but we'll stay with her no matter if it takes all day; and we'll kill her little bastards before we're through."

When Fred and Art turned to go with Red, William joined them. He had never been down in a canyon, nor had he seen a lobo's den, and he was eager to go along. The wolf led them on a wild chase across the plain. She finally—it looked as if reluctantly—ducked around a rock and headed for the canyon. Ordinarily, Fred said, a lobo could outrun any horse, but this one was so gorged that she found it impossible to make good her escape. They followed her to her den.

"Someone has to go in and rope her," Red said as they peered into the narrow cave. "No one here is small enough, except you, kid, so crawl in, Billy. After you rope her, we'll pull her out. With her taken care of, it'll be easy to get the little 'uns out."

William had no doubt that he could get through the narrow hole even though it would be a tight fit, but he did not relish the prospect of crawling upon a rattler in the dark or of being unable to move quickly if attacked by the lobo.

"I don't think I care to be cornered by a lobo or to crawl upon a rattler," he said in reply.

"Rattlers are never in the same hole as a lobo," Red informed him. "And the only thing that old she-wolf might do to you is scare you to death."

It was some time before William knew for certain that everything Red had said was correct, that the lobo was a craven coward and that, like the other four-legged animals on the plains, the antelope and the jackrabbit, it had only one means of defending itself: the ability to flee with great speed. At the moment, however, he was in no mood to test the reliability of Red's arguments, and when Red kept on needling him, he became irritated.

"If it's just someone small you want, why don't you go in yourself. You told me yesterday you weighed only a hundred and ten pounds, and even I'm heavier than that."

He could see from the faces of the other men that they expected one of Red's outbursts, but instead, Red even seemed to be enjoying himself. There was a sly smile on his lean face.

"Because I'm the boss, and you're the hand."

William stood motionless for a moment as he considered what Red had said. Red was right, and he quickly realized it. If the time of giving orders was to come, he must first learn to take them.

"I hadn't thought of it that way. I'll go," he said.

So the rope was tied around him, and William began the slow crawl into the hole. The cave was long and ran a diagonal course of several feet before making a sharp turn. Beyond was total darkness. All he could see was the bright eyes of the wolf looking straight into his, about an arm's length away. She lay very still, with her young crowded around her. Even though it was evident that she was not going to initiate a fight, he dared not attempt to rope her at such short range and without any light. Signaling to the men to pull him out, he described his dilemma and asked Red for his pistol. After crawling in again, he quickly dispatched the wolf with one shot, then tied the rope to her. The cubs were so young their eyes were not well opened, but when he attempted to pick them up, they bit and clawed viciously. All eight were finally dug out and killed. It was an exciting adventure.

That night William was walking past the wagon when he heard Art say to Fred, "Did you notice that crusty old Red and the kid this morning? He sure gave him dirt in the beginning, but I'm damned if I don't think he's come to be his favorite hand. There's not another person in the outfit that could have given him that back talk about his size without being fired. It sure puzzles me."

The wagons started rolling again after dinner to follow Red River until it turned. Then they were to cross Buck Creek into the Rockingchairs, from the Rockingchairs to the R. O.'s, and home, leaving the cattle belonging to each ranch as they went.

When they reached the Rockingchair headquarters on Little Elm, Sir Archibald rode up, spoke to his wagon boss, and rode away.

"Now ain't he the sight for sore eyes," Sam said, "a-hopping up and down on that saddle that didn't grow up? He's supposed to be Drew's chief helper, and he don't know a cow from a horse. A lot of thievin' goes on in these parts, and I ain't surprised. Them furriners that own this outfit ain't had sense enough even to register their brand, so they say, and what's a fellow to do about a stolen cow with a brand that nobody knows is official?"

In sharp contrast with the other Englishman, Alfred Rowe greeted the men cordially as they sat down together to eat dinner at the R. O. headquarters on Skillet. On seeing William, he crossed the room to shake hands with him.

"Aren't you the Lewis boy? I thought so, but you look so much like the other cowboys, I wasn't sure. Don't forget what I told you before you went to the ranch in the spring; if you ever need a job, come to see me. The R. O.'s can always use a good hand."

Their Half Circle K wagon drove into Clarendon late that afternoon. When William's mother caught the first glimpse she had had of her son in months, she threw up her hands and burst out laughing. "Good Heavens! I hardly know you. You don't look enough like the boy who went to the ranch in the spring to be kin to him. Come, stand closer. I do believe you are an inch or two taller than your father."

He was proudly aware that there were many changes in himself other than his added height. The muscles of his arms and legs were developing a slight bulge, although, in ludicrous contrast, his waist was as trim as a girl's. Above his shirt collar, his skin was burned to the hue of an Indian; there was a slight stubble on his chin, his blond hair was bleached almost white, and tiny wrinkles out from his eyes gave evidence of constant squinting against the sun's glare. His shoes were still in excellent condition, but only enough of his trousers remained to hold in place the double thickness of gunny-sacking that patched the seat.

At the end of their long talk, he said to her, "You know something, Mother: I'm going to end up with so many names, I may forget who I really am. Most everybody in the outfit calls me Will, and Red calls me Billy. But I guess as long as you and Dad keep calling me William, I'll keep feeling like William."

Sometime later his mother discovered a six-shooter among his other cowboy equipment.

1. Charles Lewis, William's father.

2. Hallie Koogle Lewis, William's mother.

4. William, about ten years old.

3. The Lewis family home and store in Frederick, Maryland.

5. William, about twenty-two years old.

6. William J. Lewis, his last photograph taken when he was about seventy-five years old.

7. Carrie Koogle, Bill's wife.

8. Sheriff Al Gentry.

9. The Rowe brothers: Alfred, *leaning on table;* Bernard, *seated;* Vincent, *on porch.*

CHAPTER XXIV

The Half Circle K outfit was to have remained in town only long enough for the boys to get a shave and haircut and to replenish their working wardrobe. To the men's and William's astonishment, they found the colony in a state of excitement and overrun with visitors. The entire court calendar had been moved up in order to bring the lease violations to trial as quickly as possible. Since many of the cowboys were to be called as witnesses, they would, of necessity, have to be on hand in Clarendon. Ranch work would have to be postponed till after the conclusion of the trial.

Both because he was curious about the nature of court procedure and because his father's name was on the docket as one of the violators, William hastened to join the spectators gathered in the courtroom the following morning. The stone building that served as the courthouse had originally been built as a hotel. The room in which court was held, having been intended for a dining room, was small. Although the crowd was not as large as he had expected, William hesitated to occupy a chair that might be needed later by some older person. Instead of sitting, he would join a young fellow, not much older than he, who was standing near the door.

It was the opening day of court. The greater part of the morning was spent impaneling the jury. It looked as if no twelve acceptable men were to be found. Everyone called was either a ranch owner or a ranch hand. As noon approached, with one juror still lacking, Judge Willis, who was plainly becoming impatient, suddenly looked hard at William and the young man next to him.[1]

Pointing to William's neighbor, he asked, "What is your name, young man?"

"Sterling P. Buster, sir."

"Do you own cattle or work on a ranch?"

"No, sir."

"Good, as of this minute you have become the twelfth juror."

[1] Willie Newbury Lewis, *Between Sun and Sod* (Clarendon: Clarendon Press, 1938), p. 213.

"But, I can't," the boy, who was clearly embarrassed, stammered. "I'm not old enough. I'm only nineteen."

"Don't talk nonsense," the judge barked back. "As of this minute I do pronounce Sterling P. Buster of legal age. Get into that jury box, and don't let me hear another word out of you."

This was not the customary procedure in a court of law, but the attorney general of the state offered no objection. He seemed as eager as the judge to get the trial under way.

William continued to stand by the door until Buster was seated in the jury box. Only then did he feel sure that the judge had not been joking. It excited him to find that there were legal means enabling a boy to reach his majority ahead of time. He left the courtroom with his thoughts busy with the future. If it were as easy as it appeared, why would he have any difficulty in doing the same thing? Maybe he was not going to have to wait as long as he had thought to own that piece of land he wanted more than anything else in the world. He must begin immediately to look around.

He returned to court after dinner with his mind made up; this time he found himself a seat, got comfortable, and settled back. The drama that unfolded during the next few days was engrossing as far as he was concerned. Because of his lack of knowledge of the customs of the Panhandle and his unfamiliarity with the legal personalities involved, he realized he probably missed many of the important implications in the actions and words of both the prosecutors and the defendants. He also realized that whatever the outcome of the trial, it would be important to the future of the ranch and of his father. He listened for hours that night as Rosie and Judge White sat around the living room table at home, discussing the ultimate effect of the trial on the Panhandle as a whole and on stock raising in particular, and describing to his father the various outsiders who were to play important parts in the trial.

He learned a great deal that night and on subsequent evenings. The prosecuting and the defense attorneys, it appeared, were among the West's outstanding lawyers.[2] Both of them had procured their

---

[2] *Ibid.*, p. 160.

legal education without benefit of books, and the rigid bar examinations that had to be passed in the East simply did not exist on the near-frontier. The qualities that had evidently been responsible for the success of the two men were common sense, experience, and a gift for pleading cases.

There was also more subtle information: Judge James U. Browning had been chosen by the ranchers as their attorney because he was a close friend of the attorney general and was the attorney general's choice to succeed Judge Willis as district judge. Equally important was the fact that Honest Jim, as Judge Browning was usually called, was a rabid reformer, who devoted his Sundays to teaching the Scripture and his weekdays to fighting two of the West's most common vices—liquor and cards. To have Honest Jim as their attorney was proof that the ranchers had moral law on their side.

Opposing him as prosecutor was handsome Judge W. H. Woodman. When Judge Woodman arose to speak, William had the feeling of being in the theatre, for the judge was every inch an actor. He was tall and had an expressive face, deep-set blue eyes, and black hair that he wore in a long bob. His hands were as beautiful as a woman's, and he used them with as much eloquence as he did his voice. He sang, implored, cajoled, wept, as the moment demanded. He rarely, it appeared, lost a case.

Judge Frank Willis, Sr., the district judge, in contrast to the two attorneys, was a legal scholar and presided at the trial with wisdom, dignity, and as much fairness as could be expected of a biased man —for the judge was on the side of the ranchmen.

With the initially entertaining showmanship of the two attorneys and the occasional restraining hand of Judge Willis, the trial began and for a while was interesting enough, quite apart from its importance to William's father and the other cattlemen—and to himself, William felt. But it dragged on and on, day after day, without any convictions. One night the jurymen, bored and eager to get home, sought a few hours' relaxation in a poker game that lasted until dawn. During the following session of court they were too fatigued to make even a pretense of being attentive. At midmorning the judge, who was also weary, called a recess. "Only a short one," he said, "but long enough for you to step over to the saloon for a drink. I am finding it particularly difficult to prove a point to jurors who are asleep in the jury box."

After the jurors had returned refreshed and were again settled in their seats, Judge Willis rose slowly to his feet. He had, he said, come to a momentous decision—one of which he knew the state attorney general would heartily disapprove, but one which had been made only after due consideration and was well within his jurisdiction. For weeks he had presided over the farcical proceedings being enacted before him. The summer session of court was proving to be a mere prolongation of the short January session. Day after day, first one cattleman and then another was tried for grazing the public domain without the payment of lease; not one conviction had resulted. To continue with cases of an identical nature was both a waste of time and a useless expenditure of state funds. The attorney general was as aware as he, the judge, that such cases would have been moved to another court had not the law decreed that the above-mentioned violation came under the category of a misdemeanor and that a misdemeanor be tried within the county in which it occurred. Any legislator should know that in a sparsely settled region like the Panhandle there were not more than fifty qualified jurors among every thousand inhabitants, and that in Donley County, of the fifty, all but a minimal few were either cattle raisers or cowboys; moreover, those not directly involved with the cattle industry would be dependent on the good will of the community for their livelihood. Furthermore, the penalty set by the state for such violations was so high as to be confiscatory. No jury in the state, be it petit or grand, would have achieved a conviction.

The judge stopped for a moment and then in a slow and drawling, but authoritative voice announced that the case on trial and all similar cases remaining on the docket were dismissed for lack of sufficient evidence.[3]

[3] The reasons that motivated Judge Willis' decision can be found in the transcript of the impeachment trial: Texas, Legislature, Senate, *Journal* 20th Leg., 1887, appendix, p. 23, found in Austin, University of Texas, Archives (Barker Historical Center).

Jumping to his feet, the infuriated, ambitious attorney general shouted, "I'll have you impeached for this"[4]

That very evening as he listened to his father and the more sober of the cattlemen, William realized that there was little cause for the jubilation of the more shortsighted ranchers. Matters were far from settled. The proceedings of the past two weeks had been little more than a preliminary skirmish to what threatened to be a prolonged fight for a way of life. It was clearly going to be the old against the new, the bold risktakers—their enemies called them "adventurers" —against the stodgy—they called themselves "settled"—citizens, the man on horseback against the man with the plough.

Gradually, as he listened more and more attentively, the whole picture of the economy of the Panhandle sharpened in outline and gained in perspective. Other indications of change took on meaning for him. He realized now, for instance, that few industries in America had arisen upon so unstable a basis and boomed in so short a time as cattle raising in the Panhandle. He gathered that the first small bunches of cattle had been turned loose on the open range by men who had become familiar with the region as they followed the buffalo across it. As cattle raising had proved more and more successful and tales of the fortunes to be made from free grass spread, another type of man had moved in, one who knew nothing about either cattle raising or the country, one whose single objective was exploitation of the land. Cattle were only a means to that end.

Both the ranches that adjoined the Half Circle K, William now realized with increased alertness, were in that category. The Heart ranch was a part of the Clarendon Land and Investment Agency. Carhart, the preacher who had established it, had sold debentures to British investors by grace of the same characteristics that he used to sell the Lord to his congregations: good looks, charm of manner, and the relentless drive of an ambitious nature. His greatest talent, like that of B. B. Groom who had established the Francklyn Land

---

[4] Judge Willis' impeachment trial was held in Austin in 1887. The judge was acquitted. When he returned to Mobeetie, his fellow citizens gave him a rousing welcome.

and Cattle Company for which the Diamond F was the brand, was a genius for promotion.

Groom, who had become manager of his company at a large salary, was a pompous Kentucky colonel who treated the cowboys as if they were stableboys and ran the business with a lavish hand. His extravagances not only headed his company toward bankruptcy, so the cattlemen and William's father felt, but made him a laughing stock all over the Texas northwest.

In the hands of two such incompetents as Carhart and Groom, the failure of their companies would have been inevitable in any case. There were now, however, difficulties that furrowed even the most competent cattlemen's brows, difficulties over which no individual had any control. In 1885, the year in which William and his family had arrived in the Panhandle, the cattle industry was at its peak. The herds of the big companies were of unbelievable size. Cattle prices were high. The big companies' profits often exceeded 40 per cent a year. In fact, everyone was prosperous, and a general air of recklessness prevailed. Then, without warning, disaster struck—first the big freeze of 1886, then a drought. The freeze, while not catastrophic, had been bad; the drought was disastrous. At the same time, the market was glutted because cattle had been shipped off hurriedly to Kansas City and Chicago since there was no grass to feed them on the plains; as a result meat prices began to fall. They were at an all-time low by the time the trial began.

"It is the end of an era," William's father said at the dinner table, "and I predict that the men who are able to go on will be the few who learn businesslike methods. I heard today that Groom has been replaced by a man named Tyng, a good and sharp Yankee, so they say; also, that the British investors are sending an Irishman, a Count Kearney, over to investigate the affairs of the Clarendon Land and Investment Agency and the Heart outfit. What is going to happen to the Half Circle K—and to us—only time will tell."

CHAPTER XXV

Although William was aware that all was not well with the ranch, he had little time to dwell on problems other than those that had to do with the daily routine, among other things the wolves that were proving to be even more troublesome than usual this fall. Because lobo had always frequented the cliffs around the Salt Fork headwaters, Sugg, shortly before selling the ranch, had purchased four very fine Siberian bloodhounds to aid in eradicating the menace. The dogs functioned well until spring and roundup time. During one of the outfit's many absences from headquarters, they wandered off to join the wolf pack. The crossbreeding resulted in a much bolder and more vicious animal than found in any other part of the Panhandle. The bolder ones often ran a calf into the corral to maim it. It was necessary to keep a constant lookout for the invaders.

It was not the wolves, however, that were the chief worry. It was the constant threat of fire. Prairie fires, which were never uncommon, were the stockman's main dread at all times. On a drought-blighted range the danger was many times multiplied. The entire country was a tinderbox. One stroke of lightning or one careless gesture on the part of a single cowboy could produce a holocaust.

The drought was in its second year, and in most places the grass had already taken on the sere and brown look of winter. There was one area, however, where, even though not green, the grass was still tall and thick: this was the open country around McClelland Creek, where many of the cows and calves were pastured. As a starting point for the fall rounding of the free grass area adjoining the ranch, the wagon camped one night in early October along one of the tributary creeks. On the following morning the boys arose, breakfasted, and rode off, leaving everything supposedly in good order. Who was responsible for the catastrophe that followed no one ever knew. They could only surmise from Boney's account that someone had accidentally dropped a burning cigarette into his bed as he rolled it up, preparatory to placing it in the wagon. There the cigarette smoldered till long after the last rider was gone from camp.

Only the cook and a new and inexperienced youngster who had recently joined the outfit remained behind. Being busy, they failed to notice anything until it was too late. By the time they caught the first whiff of smoke, the wagon was already on fire, with its entire contents ready to burst into flames. The grass, ignited by sparks and by burning bits of the canvas wagon top, caught like kindling. Minutes after the first spark hit the ground, the line of fire was spreading in all directions.

"There's no stopping it," Boney had shouted to his bewildered assistant. "Unstake the horses, and we'll try to get 'em across that draw about three miles from here, and just hope the fire don't jump it. Anyway, unless they run into the Diamond F fence, they can keep ahead of it, maybe. After that we'd better get the hell away ourselves."

The entire pasture was aflame before the boys who were off rounding noticed the smoke and located one another.

"It's traveling about fifteen miles an hour," Red said, "and headed straight across the Diamond F corner into the ranch. Our only chance to save the Half Circle K is to get a strip burned out ahead of it. I just saw a few head of cattle a mile back where we came from. Get 'em rounded and we'll go to work."

Having collected the cattle, and reached a location far enough in advance of the conflagration to provide time and safety, the men divided into teams. Some ignited a long line of grass while others hastened to slaughter the small bunch of recently rounded cattle. Each cow was split down the back. As soon as an area of sufficient size to stop the progress of the fire was completely burned, two riders began dragging a bleeding carcass, with a foreleg tied to each horse, over the flames at the outer edges. Art Sherrod and William followed behind with saddle blankets to beat out the remaining patches of burning grass. Everyone worked steadily throughout the day, stopping only to take his turn at getting a short respite from the smoke and heat.

Sometime during the afternoon William became separated from Art. He was still working alone when the incident that almost cost him his life occurred. Everything went as expected until the approach of night. A strong wind suddenly arose, causing the fire to spread rapidly and to take unexpected directions. Realizing that he could not handle the situation without assistance, William decided to ride back in search of Art.

As he walked toward Pony, a fence of which he had not been aware came unexpectedly into view a short distance ahead of him. There was no doubt he had come to the Diamond F pasture. It surprised him to learn he had covered such a distance since noon. Still unaware of the danger of his situation, he unstaked Pony and had a foot in the stirrup when the crackling of newly ignited grass aroused his suspicions. He turned to take a look and saw the burning plain. There was not one line of moving fire; there were two, and they extended from the point at which they met all the way back to the fence. He was completely enclosed in a triangle formed from one barbed wire fence and two fast-encroaching walls of flame. Apparently all avenues of escape were already closed. It would take too long to get the fence down, and there was not a second to lose. If he and Pony were to get out of this alive, something must be done immediately without considering the hazards or the cost. Their only possible route of escape was directly through the fire.

With his decision made, William hastily threw the blanket with which he had been working over the pony's head. At the first whiff of scorched wool, Pony became fractious. William hesitated only long enough to give him a few reassuring pats and to say, "Calm down, old boy. Don't you know I wouldn't do this if I didn't have to, and this time give me all you've got, for what you do in the next minute will mean your life as well as mine."

Then, with the bridle held tightly in one hand and the blanket in the other, William leaned forward in the saddle and gave a swift dig with his heels into the pony's sides. Pony, already headed in the right direction, jumped forward and started running, with William urging him on. Straight into the flames they went—flames that sometimes reached the saddle horn—through the burning grass and out onto the open plain and safety.

Once beyond the terrific heat, William brought Pony to a stop and dismounted, pulling the blanket off as he went. With no concern for himself, he turned his attention to his frantic horse. He found upon examination that the left eye had been injured. His forelegs and shoulders were badly burned, and most of the hair on his body was singed off. It would be months before he could be ridden again.

A sobered and thankful youngster began to walk back. William had suffered slight injury. Only his hands were burned. He found the men still fighting. The fire lasted until almost morning when a shift in the wind stopped its spread. By that time, it had burned for a distance of forty miles, across one corner of the Diamond F and the entire length of the Half Circle K.

There was little sleep that night. Notwithstanding, by daylight Boney and his helper had gone for a new wagon and supplies and the other men were ready to gather and count the horses and cattle that had escaped the prairie fire. When that was done, the rounding of the free grass areas began again. The steers were turned loose outside the ranch to forage as best they could till spring; the good cows were left on McClelland, where the grass was fair; the thin ones or the ones that had calved late were placed on the always thick and rich grasses of Boggy.

CHAPTER XXVI

The "hay meadow," as the pasture on the Boggy was called, lay to the north of the Clarendon settlement, between the spring-fed Allen Creek and its small tributary the Boggy, from which the region derived its name. Because of ever-present subsurface moisture, both tule and three-cornered water grass grew in such abundance that a hay crop was harvested twice a year. Like all the McClelland Creek country, of which it was a part, it was generally considered to be Half Circle K property although, in reality, it was one of the numerous school sections, which, in alternating with the sections purchased from the railroad, gave the actual ranch property an impractical serrated boundary line.[1] To obviate the difficulty,

---

[1] The Panhandle was surveyed in alternate sections—one school, one rail-

Koogle had not hesitated to follow the accepted practice of enclosing land belonging to the state along with his own. It was violations such as this which had instigated the passage of the lease laws and had also brought Goodnight and the other ranchers to trial.

Of all this, William was growing increasingly conscious. It was important to him because these sections were among the few places where the grass grew green and thick even during a drought and where thin cows never failed to fatten when wintered there. He thought often of the weeks he had spent there in the spring, of little Birl and the heel flies, and of the many things that had happened since.

One day while he was riding alone behind Red and Art, with his thoughts on the cattle he hoped to have, William was sharply brought back to the present on hearing the word "Boggy" and the foreman's voice, as Red went on talking.

"There ain't another pasture like it on the ranch, and wouldn't you think that after three years Koogle would have got around to havin' someone file on it for him? How do you reckon the Diamond F straightened out their boundary line? Not by buying the school sections, I can tell you, but by refusing to hire anyone unless he filed and promised to turn the located land over to the ranch at the end of the first year. The Half Circle K looks like a broken-toothed comb all around the edges, but Bill Koogle don't have time to do anything about it. He's too busy drinkin' and gamblin' and playin' the big cow man. Now it's too late. They've passed a law against sellin' to the outfit you work for, and the first thing you know some smart farmer's goin' to get that land and move our cattle off."

William rode on behind them in silence, his mind hard at work. All at once, he knew exactly what to do with the money he had won at the races. He would have to talk to his father, of course; but someone must do something to save the hay meadow for the ranch! That day marked the end of the roundup, and he rode into town to stay until the spring work began in April.

---

road section. The railroad sections were purchasable, but the school sections were for settlements.

The Clarendon settlement, like other parts of the Panhandle, was in a period of transition. Leigh Dyer's proposal to change the survey had been accepted by the railroad company. After years of delay, the Fort Worth and Denver was rushing construction by laying track from both ends of the line. The westerly division had reached the Red River, and the juncture between the two divisions was to be effected by late summer of the following year.

A meeting between the Clarendon representatives and the railroad officials took place in September to discuss the "new Clarendon." The officials proposed to make the location a division point, provided sufficient land for a town adjoining the railroad was made available to them without cost. The townspeople agreed, but with the stipulation that four hundred of the choicest lots be reserved for those desirous of changing their residence and place of business from the old to the new town. The location decided upon was near the small lake William and his parents had passed shortly before reaching the Clarendon colony. Some difficulty was encountered in persuading the owner of the property involved to sell to a "lot of damn Yankees," as he called the promoters, but with Rosie's assistance the deal was finally concluded.

A mad scramble for lots began as soon as the townsite officials made public the location of the depot. It was the desire of every merchant to be as close to the railroad as possible. Immediately, the firm of Wood and Dickson, which owned a chain of frontier stores, began work on a store that would operate a banking department as well as sell dry goods and groceries. Rosenfield, who was severing the partnership with Judge White, procured for his new store a large corner lot directly opposite the supposed depot site and hastily started construction on the building. He had no intention of being done in by his important rivals.

From that time on, little business was transacted in the old Clarendon. Only the ranches continued to buy as before; the other customers were in the mood only for the bare necessities, and the interest of the merchants themselves was largely centered on their future in the new town.

William's father and Ralph were out of town most of the time although as yet their plans were not definite enough for the purchase of a lot. During their absence William was left in charge of both the post office and the combined stores. One morning while he was straightening the bolts of material on the shelves, a young man came in and, without speaking, started to rummage through the merchandise. Since this was not unusual and since the man looked like a cowboy, although his complexion was less weathered than most cowboys', William glanced at him only once and then went on with his work. Just about the time he had finished with the shelves, he saw the stranger walk to a counter on which some wearing apparel, spurs, and an extra good leather belt were on display. He picked up the spurs and belt, pulled a piece of paper from his pocket, and turned to William.

With an air of confidence, he pointed to the paper and said, "This is a check on the Rafter Eye. I'm kin to old Noah Ellis and work for him. Tie the package up good for I've got a long ride ahead."

The purchase was sizable, and William was pleased to make the sale. With the nearest bank at Harrold and very little currency in circulation, checks were the accepted way of payment. While the boy was adding up the amounts of the various things the man had bought, it came to him that only a few years ago when he first arrived here with his parents, he was as cautious as the people in the East; now, like any Westerner, he was willing to take any man's honesty for granted until there was evidence to the contrary.

He tied up all the purchases with a strong cord, took the check, gave the man two dollars and forty cents in change, thanked him and bade him good-bye. He was still pleased with himself when he glanced once more at the check before tucking it into the cash drawer. Soon, however, a vague uneasiness came over him; for reasons he could not explain, he felt something was wrong.

Hurriedly he locked the store and rushed out to find Rosie, who happened not to be out of town. When told the story, Rosie said: "You've been taken in by a crook. Old Noah Ellis used to bring cattle in, but he left here long before any of us reached the Panhandle. He never owned the Rafter Eye Ranch. Don't take it too hard; the best way to learn is from experience. You'll know better next time."

CHAPTER XXVII

The bad-check incident happened in December. It wasn't long before it was Christmas and then New Year's Day of 1887. A week later, court was in session.

One morning as he passed Judge Willis on the street, William was forcibly reminded of his intention to take up the land around Boggy so potentially valuable to the ranch. He hesitated, however, to approach the judge, so decided to discuss the matter with his father before doing anything about it.

That evening when the subject was broached, his father suggested an idea that had never occurred to William. "I feel certain son," he said, "that the judge would not only be willing to help you but would be able to find a way. But why do it in such a round-about way? You get along so well with your cousin Bernie and he is always more than willing to do anything you suggest. He was twenty-one a few months ago. Why don't you and Bernie take up the land together?"

By nightfall William was at Bernie's house, and Bernie was enthusiastic over the plan. He had more than enough cash saved to make his half of the initial payment to the state, and he agreed that the job of sleeping the required number of nights on the property and of breaking the required number of acres would not be too hard with two of them to do it. But Bernie's father would not hear of it for a while; there was no time, he claimed, for Bernie to be away, even for just a day or two. In the end, however, swayed by their enthusiasm and by William's description of Boggy, Mr. Rhoderick relented.

Within four days, all the details had been attended to and the names of William Lewis and Bernie Rhoderick were being registered in Austin as those of the settlers on seven sections of the choicest land in the Panhandle.

William was triumphant. His elation warmed him inside all through the winter. He thought of their lush sections on Boggy at home, in the store, before going to sleep, and the first thing when he awakened in the morning.

CHAPTER XXVIII

Early in the new year, the box car that was to serve as the temporary depot was rolled into position beside the Fort Worth and Denver tracks, not, however, at the location previously designated. Wood and Dickson found themselves on a back street, and Rosie's predicament was even worse. His store was a good quarter of a mile from the new center of town. The townsite officials declined to set forth their reasons for the change of plans and remained adamant to the pleas of the irate merchants.

As soon as the depot dispute seemed settled, William's cousin Ralph purchased fifty-five feet in the center of the west side of the newly named Main Street. For once, his procrastination had served him well.

With the coming of spring, William returned to the ranch to work —not as the boss's son and a mere apprentice cowboy this time, but as a seasoned hand. Although the bitter weather of the preceding years and the lack of moisture had cut the herd by one fourth, the same routine as always was necessary. Moreover, general conditions were somewhat improved. Cattle prices, while still low, had ceased their downward slide, and, after twenty-three months, the drought was finally broken. Refreshed by the seasonal rains of May, even the burned-over range was showing green.

William did not get into town again until late in July when the wagon was sent in to give assistance in turning the Heart outfit over to the receiver at the insistence of the British investors. By the morning of the first roundup, both Preacher Carhart and the ranch foreman had left town. Not only all the American creditors were present, among them the representative of the Brush estate, the banker from Iowa who had assisted Koogle financially in the purchase of the Half Circle K Ranch, but so were many of the big cattle operators. It was the first time a large ranch had gone into the hands of the receiver. Everybody in the Panhandle was intent on the proceedings. Only Koogle was absent. It was a serious business, William slowly realized, indicative of a changing era. It also afforded fun and excitement for everybody who lived within driving distance of Clarendon.

Buggies and wagons started for the roundup pasture early in the morning, to assure each family a timely arrival. For the first time in months, the new town was not the main point of interest. Each day at noon the entire population of the colony enjoyed their midday meal at one of the three wagons handling the roundup—the Heart wagon, or the J. A., or that of the Half Circle K.

By the end of the fortnight, the business of turning the Heart Ranch over to the receiver and the creditors was finished. A cattle operation that had sprung from the wild dream of a country preacher and had grown into a reality involving untold acres of land and thirty thousand head of cattle had been liquidated. The visitors from out of town were gone, and the townspeople were back at their prosaic tasks.

The only visitor who did not leave was the banker from Iowa. With the unfortunate Heart Ranch business behind him, J. H. Brush's attention was focused on his other endangered loan, that of the Half Circle K. He clearly hoped in this case to avoid the sort of loss he had just suffered. He had called for a meeting with William's father and the two other Half Circle K partners.

At the hour set for the meeting, William's father—William had been allowed to come with him—was the only one of the three partners who put in an appearance at the B. H. White and Company store. Ralph had refused, even as a courtesy, to relinquish his role of silent partner, and Koogle, the actual manager of the ranch, as usual, could not be located. Rosie and Judge White were with Brush when William followed his father through the door of the store.

"I can readily understand your failure to find him," the banker said when William's father apologized for the absence of his brother-in-law, "for he never seems to be in any one spot for long. Apparently my letters never reach him; anyway, they are never answered, and his telegrams come from the most unexpected places."

The banker paused for a minute and shuffled some papers.

"I think it may be just as well that you, the judge, Rosie, and I have a meeting without him. I have asked them both to be present because they know more about general conditions and the people around here than anyone else in the Panhandle. Business has been bad during the last two years for all cattlemen, and the time has come when I must know about the operation of your ranch and about the man who supposedly is running it."

"I surmised as much," William's father said, "so I took the liberty of bringing someone with me—my son. You may have seen him before. Don't be misled by his youth. He thinks straight, and he has been with the outfit through the working season for two years. He can tell you more about the range, the cattle, and the way things have been managed than I can. It was never planned for me to do anything but keep the books. Bill's reticence about business he considers personal and his aversion to keeping accurate records have made my task an impossible one. I hope sincerely that I, as well as you, shall learn much from today's conference."

The talk lasted until late afternoon. William listened intently; he was fascinated by what he heard, but his uneasiness grew as he began to realize that this was also the first time that all the details of the ranch business had been revealed to his father. The profit counted on from pasturing the Spur herd of more than five thousand head of cattle and the slightly smaller herd owned by Koogle himself and by his wife's brother-in-law Corrigan had been greatly reduced by the loss of a large number of cattle in the freeze. The misadventure of the Tandy cattle also was gone into by the men, and here and on other occasions William was proud to be asked by the banker for details. But he was dismayed to learn that Koogle had convinced his partners to sign another Brush loan in 1886 for $15,000; the money had been used to purchase cattle to replace those lost in the freeze. All in all, as the long day wore on, the picture was not one to inspire confidence either in Bill Koogle as a manager or in the Half Circle K as a sound business investment.

Although William knew that his father was deeply shocked by the day's revelations, he gathered from the conversation that there were a few encouraging sides to the situation. To begin with, the Brush loan had more than two years to go. With the drought at last at an end and cattle prices rising steadily, there was a chance of saving the ranch, given a little time and a modicum of luck.

One thing was clear to both of them: whatever was done would have to be done by them, without help from either of the other partners. William caught his father looking at him once and saw an expression on his face he had never seen before—a look of helplessness, as if his father were turning to him for protection. A sudden surge of emotion swept over him. There was no doubt it was he alone, a mere boy of seventeen, upon whom his father was placing the responsibility of saving the ranch.

On the slow walk home neither spoke.

CHAPTER XXIX

On 9 September 1887, after William and the rest of the Half Circle K outfit had already returned to the ranch to finish the fall work, the two divisions of the Fort Worth and Denver met near the new town. It was an event not to be missed. The whole outfit rode in from the ranch for the festivities. The driving-in of the golden spike was celebrated with a barbecue and numerous speeches by railroad officials and prominent townspeople. William enjoyed it all. Even the high-flown or stumbling and always lengthy speeches were a break in the usually uneventful flow of life in the town. Afterwards there was a dance.

There was much to celebrate. The stock pens were ready for use. Freight service was to begin within a few days, and the first passenger run was promised for early October. Sixty miles to the northwest, at the place where the Southern Kansas Railroad would bisect the Fort Worth and Denver, a new town called Amarillo had been established, thus putting the Clarendon cattlemen within easy shipping distance of Chicago and Kansas City.

William watched with fascination the many shifts and changes brought about by the coming of the railroad. So far the only fully completed building in town was that of the Wood and Dickson firm. Although Ralph had ordered the lumber as soon as the lot was purchased, the problems of freighting it in and of finding skilled labor had caused him to delay starting his building until after the beginning of train service. William was much pleased by the prospective plans as described to him by his father. The lot was 125 feet deep. Because of the small space required by the post office, there would be ample room for both the mailboxes and the dry goods counters of William's father on one side and for Ralph's grocery store on the other. The plans also showed a four-room apartment upstairs for Ralph's family and two extra bedrooms at the back to be rented.

Meanwhile, William's parents, who had secured a homestead lot in the new town, decided to continue living in old Clarendon until after the store was well established, a decision influenced largely by their desire not to leave Em alone in her old-Clarendon house while Ralph was busy with the construction of his new building, six miles away.

By November every merchant had something under way. A few of the smaller stores went up quickly, but larger buildings like Ralph's progressed so slowly that it was still anybody's guess as to when they would be ready for occupancy. Meanwhile a whole tent city sprang up along the tracks. It was a completely new town, different in every way from the old Clarendon on Salt Fork. Each train brought an influx of strangers, most of whom belonged to the railroad crews. They were a tough, hard-working, hard-drinking lot. The new town had none of the restrictions that Carhart had attempted to impose on the old Clarendon. A separate tent city known as Feather Hill and inhabited only by girls, bartenders, and gamblers, occupied the slight rise to the east. Every fourth citizen of the new town was a gambler, and every other businessman was the proprietor of a saloon.

William's father and Ralph, like the other merchants, had opened for business in a tent until the store could be built. Although Em had moved in with William's mother in the old town, William's father insisted that William stay with them after he was through with the fall work at the ranch, except on weekends when he took over at the tent store, so that his father and Ralph could go home for a day or so. The distance was too great—a good six miles over next to no road —for the two men to ride back and forth every day, and someone had to be in the store constantly.

It was a difficult time for all of them, William realized, and an extremely dull period for him, since during the long summer season with the ranch outfit, he had become accustomed to having every minute of the day filled. One morning, chafing at his boredom, he had a sudden idea for putting his enforced leisure to profitable use. There was a scarcity of firewood and water in the new Clarendon, and a scarcity of provisions in the old colony.

At this time the mail was still being delivered by a freighter to the old colony. It was William's job twice a week to take it over to the tent store, which was serving as a temporary post office. It occurred to him that if he could get Bernie to help, it would pay them well to rent a wagon and transport water and firewood to the new Clarendon on the days the mail was delivered there and to return by the old colony with the wagon loaded with the staples necessary to the remaining housewives and the occasional passing rancher. Bernie was agreeable to the plan.

They lost no time in renting a wagon and found no difficulty in getting one dollar a barrel for water in the new town. With their recently acquired stock, they opened for business in Ralph's abandoned post office. There was a good profit in the potatoes, beans, flour, and even notions they had for sale. The weeks were suddenly no longer dreary, and the weekends in the new town offered the excitement the now largely deserted old Clarendon lacked.

The new town, William was told by an elderly railroad man who dropped in to buy some chewing tobacco at the tent store, was a typical rough and roistering railroad settlement. All William knew was that during the weeks following the coming of the Fort Worth and Denver, Clarendon as a community had deteriorated steadily in character. The former "colonists," as Carhart had called them, formed only a small part of the population now, and many of the newcomers were of an entirely different type. The most lucrative hours for business were after dark when the freely spending section workers and trainmen were at leisure. They were well paid and very much alike in the desire to gamble and drink away the wages they had labored strenuously to earn. In addition, there were the trail drivers, whose sizable orders were eagerly sought and who always drove in at night, demanding service, no matter what the hour. It was thus necessary to have someone behind the counter around the clock, day and night, to protect the cash in the store as well as to handle the trade.

A bank had recently been opened in the new little town of Carson City, about 30 miles away. Although the distance was not nearly so great as the 130 miles to Harrold had been, it was still too far to make frequent deposits practical. As a result, many merchants and ranchers kept large sums of money on hand, either in ducking sacks or in a belt around the waist. Nearly every house and store in town was a depository of sorts. William's father and uncle kept their cash in a small sack hidden among the many packages of coffee in a case behind the counter. William soon had good reason to become more than usually aware of the valuable sack.

One gray November morning when he was working in the tent store to give his father a chance to make a necessary trip to the ranch, a telegram arrived with the news that Em's father was seriously ill in Washington. Ralph left hurriedly to make sure of having his wife in town by train time the next day. His absence meant that William had sole responsibility of the store for the next twenty-four hours. He did not mind; it was no more than he faced every weekend. It was fun, except that business was brisk and there was not even a minute's relief until on into the night. He barely found time to make a couple of sandwiches from the bread and cheese and cold beef his mother had insisted that he take along—and barely time to eat them.

When the town finally began to settle down for the night, about two o'clock, William decided to close up for a few hours of sleep. He tied the tent strings, put out the lamps, and, as he did on Saturdays and Sundays, climbed without undressing up on the counter, which, with a pillow and a blanket, had to serve as his bed. He had been warned about attempts at robbery but had never considered it necessary to have a gun close at hand all the time. Mindful, however, that there was an unusually large amount of cash in the sack, he placed Ralph's pistol under his pillow.

He had been asleep only a few minutes seemingly, when he awakened with the uncanny feeling that someone else was in the tent. He opened his eyes and, without moving his head, looked as far as was possible, to either side. It was bright moonlight outside, and a narrow stream of light came through the tent opening, which was not fully closed. Evidently, someone had untied the flap. In the semidarkness William was able to make out the form of a man moving cautiously behind the far counter, groping along, as if in search of something he expected to find under the counter or somewhere in the pile of merchandise on top.

William's heart beat fast, and an uneasy feeling arose in his stomach. He had faced wild broncs, rattlesnakes, and stampeding cattle without an undue amount of fear. But at no other time in his life had he felt as defenseless as he felt before the stranger behind the counter. His feelings, however, were of little importance. The man was up to no good, and he must be stopped before it was too late.

As quietly as possible, William pulled the pistol from under the pillow. Holding it firmly in his hands, he eased his legs off the counter, then jumped to his feet. The robber did not attempt to escape on seeing the gun, as William had expected him to do. Instead, he moved toward the exit, mumbling and stumbling in the manner of one too drunk to know where he was or what he was doing. On reaching the street, he straightened up and ran.

As he went through the opening, William, who was still standing motionless, caught a good look at his face in the moonlight. To his surprise, William saw that the fellow resembled one of the railroad workers whom he often saw around town but whose name he did not know.

It was then four o'clock. William tied the tent flap once more and crawled back on the counter, but this time he put the gun within easy reach. Tired as he was, he could not go to sleep. He kept going over and over the events of the night. He was angry with himself for his lack of composure, and he went hot with shame when he remembered that his hand with the pistol had shaken so badly he would have missed his mark even if he had fired a shot. The only thing that cheered him was the thought that nothing had been stolen, and he felt relieved that he had not pulled the trigger even though his not doing so had permitted the man to escape. All the same, he must be better prepared next time. He resolved to wear his gun constantly and, as often as he could find time, to practice the gunman's quick draw. In this, too, he must become expert! He slept fitfully for a few hours.

CHAPTER XXX

In the morning, Ralph returned to the store after putting Em on the train for Washington. Since his father was expected in that afternoon, William left at once for the old town to be with his mother. For a few days everything went on as usual. But the end of the week when he returned to Clarendon for the weekend, he found both his father and the tent store in a state of confusion. Without warning, Ralph had returned to his former habits. There were saloons on all sides, and, with Em gone, Ralph was suddenly spending all his time in them.

Aware that he could not handle the store alone, William's father had no choice but to make William take Ralph's place. Since William's mother and sister, unlike the men, could not camp in a tent, and since as yet there was no suitable place in town for them to stay until the new family cottage was built (and plans for this were still indefinite), the only alternative was for them to remain alone in the house on the Salt Fork. The old Clarendon was by now practically deserted. Only Corbett, the bootmaker, Professor Combs and his wife, and three families from the Heart Ranch were left. It was not a pleasant prospect for the women; it worried his father, William knew, but there was no other way. It was one more hardship they had to face.

Christmas came—Christmas of 1887, the year of the coming of the railroad, as everyone thought of it. To avoid the presence of the rougher element among the newcomers, the former colonists decided to hold their Christmas celebration in the deserted saloon back in the old town, as they had always done in previous years. The owners of all the adjoining ranches were to be present, too. It was a much anticipated event, more like a homecoming and family reunion than anything else.

When the evening came, everyone was in fine spirits and full of conversation. Rosenfield was first on the program that had been planned for the after-supper entertainment. Rosie had sung only a few bars when the clatter of boots and loud voices announced the arrival of Ralph and Koogle. They were disheveled and so intoxicated that neither could stand without assistance from the other. William and his father hurried over to them but could not persuade them to be quiet or to leave. As no performer was able to compete with their boisterous words and laughter, the evening came to an early close. Out of respect for the families involved, the other guests dispersed without more ado.

Before the end of the holidays, Ralph's building was ready for occupancy. The first few months of the New Year were to bring many changes to the family. As quickly as possible Ralph and his son Harry settled themselves in the apartment, and the move from the tent store to permanent quarters was begun. Although the store did not open for business for several days, the post office was put in operation immediately.

William moved into one of the back bedrooms. Much to his delight, he found that his roommate was the gambler, Bill Menasco, who was one of the two gamblers who had opened the saloon in the old town shortly after the arrival of William and his parents. Menasco was a settled and experienced man of the world, and William enjoyed his company greatly. Furthermore, William felt that he would always be indebted to him, for it was Menasco who forced Gatherin to pay for the return of the lost mules. William often lay on his cot by the window and looked across into the saloon where he could see Menasco at his table. He was a well-educated and well-mannered man, and William could not understand why he followed a profession that William held in low esteem.

The gambler had been his roommate for only a few days when the first blizzard of the year blew in. Although the storm was not as severe or as prolonged as the ones of the previous winters, it hit just as suddenly and as savagely. William had driven in from delivering groceries only a few minutes before, without a coat. Fearing for the safety of his mother and sister, who were alone in the house on the

Salt Fork, he saddled hastily and set out for the old town. It was already dusk. The wind tore viciously across the plain, and the air was thick with stinging particles of ice. He had not ridden more than a mile when he realized that he could never make it to the river, and across, alive; he could not stay in the saddle without freezing. To attempt to reach the old town on foot would be just as suicidal. There was only one thing to do; he dismounted and turned his horse loose, hoping that instinct would take the pony back to town; then in a dog-trot to keep his circulation moving, he started back the way he had come. The gale became fiercer and icier by the minute; it was hard just to get enough breath. His arms were numb by the time he finally got to the store. The horse had beaten him in.

No one slept that night. Bundled in blankets, they sat around a roaring fire. The temperature, a few steps away, was that of the out-of-doors. It was noon of the following day before William and his father considered it safe to travel, and midafternoon before they reached the house across the river. Their fears had been needless. When they walked in, they found William's mother baking a cake.

"Certainly, we were uneasy," she admitted. "No one relishes being made a prisoner. We knew we couldn't get to our neighbors, nor could they get to us; but we were well sheltered and we had ample food and water. As you see, we're in good health and, I hope, spirits. Firewood was our only problem."

"That's what worried me most," William's father said. "I knew the wood pile was 'way back from the house. What did you do?"

"Oh, it was simple. I couldn't see a foot in front of me; so to make sure I could get back, I tied one end of a rope William had luckily left here around my waist, and the other end to a back porch post. I wandered around a little before I could find the wood pile, but once there, it was easy to follow the rope back to the house. I made several trips."

"I'll be damned," said his father, who was not given to swearing. "I suppose pioneers are born, not made. In the same circumstances, I'd probably have frozen to death."

There were, however, two minor catastrophes. The shelves and shelves of preserves his mother had made during the summer had burst, and the two milk cows when finally found were still standing, but frozen stiff.

Three days later, the news came that Em's father had died. Instead of announcing her immediate return, she wrote that she was planning to stay on for the settlement of the estate, possibly for a period of several months. That the inheritance was of great importance to her, they all well knew. With Ralph doing more and more drinking and the ranch threatened with failure, the inheritance was Em's only certain means of support. William's parents, however, had been wondering for some time whether she would not return East eventually anyway. She was disappointed in her marriage, and they felt that she must have concluded long ago that she was waging a losing battle in her struggle to save her husband from his addiction and that her years of loneliness and sacrifice had been in vain.

At the same time, William's father discovered that by paying an exorbitant price he would be able to rent for his family a recently completed three-room house in town. Since the life of the family required more than three rooms, he hastily began building a large kitchen, which he planned to join temporarily to the rent house by a passageway and later to move for permanence as a necessary part of the family's new home whenever it was built. As soon as the kitchen was finished, the family moved.

They were scarcely settled in the new town when Harry Jefferson took a long and imprudent walk across the river and contracted the cold that ended his life. His death was so sudden that there was not time to notify Em or to get her back to Clarendon. At her request, her son's body was returned to Washington for burial. There was no mention made of Em's return. Ralph was now alone. There was no longer any restraining influence upon him, and as the months went by his problem increased. As a result, William's father had the triple responsibility of the ranch, the store, and the post office.

It was not long after William's mother and sister had settled in the new Clarendon when Katie was offered the job of writing the many official records kept by Tom Martindale, the county clerk. It was she who wrote many of Goodnight's deeds and contracts. Occasionally she was called on to act as substitute teacher in the new school. Her leisure was kept busy by her new suitor, Ben Chamberlain.

It fell to William's lot to serve as the store's chief clerk. Although, like his father, he was inclined to be reserved and without the easy chattiness of many of their customers, he liked people and could not fail to notice that they seemed to like him. He realized that something about the way he looked and about his manner belied his essentially shy and ingrown nature. It had not taken him long to discover that his readiness to listen, even though he had little to say in return, and his willingness to make himself useful in small ways was appreciated by people. Above all, they seemed to value his gift for remembering faces and names and their different preferences and requirements. Occasional compliments came his way, and, although the only praise that had ever made him flush with pleasure had been Red's grudging admission that he was "all right" and the wordless acceptance of him by the seasoned cowboys as an equal, he was warmed by the realization that he had a reputation for being responsible and hardworking and that he seemed to be something of a general favorite in the town, especially with the old Clarendon residents and with the ranchers.

Among the latter, very important group of customers was Alfred Rowe[1] the courteous and pleasant Englishman who owned the ranch below the cap rock. The R.O.'s, as the ranch was called, was rolling prairie land, well watered by the Salt Fork and its tributaries and protected from the severe northern winds by the cap rock escarpment. On the rare occasions when William had time to dream, he

[1] Willie Newbury Lewis, *Between Sun and Sod* (Clarendon: Clarendon Press, 1938), p. 108. Alfred Rowe arrived in Donley County the year after the establishment of the colony. Through the purchase of railroad scrip, he established himself to the north of Skillet Creek. (It is possible there was a block of school land included in this tract.) There, in a two-room sod house covered with shingles freighted in from Dodge City, he set up his first headquarters. He later bought the White Fish property from Carhart and Sully. Sometime later Alfred was joined by his two brothers, Bernard and Vincent, who bought one-third interest in the ranch. Later this interest was returned to Alfred. His two brothers did not remain in Texas.

always thought of the R.O.'s. It was perfect cow country, exactly the kind of ranch he would own one day if his plans worked out.

The Englishman was a friend of William's parents, and William felt that Rowe liked him. When he came into the store, Rowe never failed to spend some time with him, and it was quite clear to William that the R.O. Ranch had become the very symbol of what he wanted, and the gentleman-rancher, so different in every way from the other cattlemen, the symbol of the ideal ranch owner. Some day, the boy continued to dream, he too would own acres and acres of beautiful rolling land and on the creeks and in the draws would be hundreds and hundreds of cows and calves, and on each one would be a brand that was his, and his alone.

CHAPTER XXXI

There was, however, little time to daydream, for the work around the store was never at an end. One morning during a slight lull William went to the back to clean the gun he had worn ever since the episode in the tent store. He had proceeded no further than unloading it, breaking it, and removing the cylinder, when he heard the door up front open and slam to. Putting the dismantled gun on a box, he hurried to the front. The man who stood facing him was the cowboy who had defrauded him back in the old town.

The mere sight of the cowboy and his insolence in daring to come into the store infuriated William. He asked to be paid at once for the bad check.

The cowboy only laughed at him, "I didn't come in either to buy something or to pay for something I already have. I just dropped in to see if movin' from the Salt Fork into town was helpin' a smart-alec kid to wise up."

William had never thought of himself as quick and hot-tempered. Once aroused, however, as he was now, his fury knew no bounds, and he was ready to take on anyone, even a tough saddle tramp twice his age and size. The cowboy, openly amused at the violent reaction of an opponent who apparently presented very little danger became increasingly abusive. Through his harangue, William stood silent and taut. Then the cowboy made one taunt too many. At the words "little boy" something in William snapped, and he charged at him. The man stumbled backward with a stupid look of surprise on his face. For a few seconds William enjoyed the sensation of having dealt a crook the punishment he deserved. In those seconds, however, the cowboy managed to straighten up and, having regained his balance, to deal William a blow that sent him reeling all the way back against the grocery counter. He tried to catch hold of the edge of the counter to keep from falling but failed. As his hand slid along the top, it came in contact with one of the weights for the scale; he grasped it tightly, at the same time propping himself against the counter. When the cowboy came rushing at him, he struck out wildly. The man crumpled to the floor.

While he was standing over him, stunned by what he had done, Menasco ran in, shouting as he came, "What the hell's going on? You can hear the commotion clear to the saloon door where I was standing."

On seeing the unconscious man on the floor, he said hurriedly, "Don't stop to tell me anything. Just get the doctor as fast as you can. When you get back, I'll go after the sheriff. I'll tell him I came in just as it happened, that you were unarmed, and that when you saw the cowboy reach for his gun, you hit him with the first thing that was handy."

Because the blow had been a serious one to the head, the doctor refused to make any prognosis. At the doctor's suggestion, the injured man was moved to a bed upstairs. Then the long wait began.

News of the fight spread fast. Even before the sheriff came, the store was filled with people. Before William could answer the sheriff's first question, the gambler interrupted.

"Here, let me tell the story. The boy doesn't know as well as I what happened. I was standing in the saloon door when I heard the noise. I ran right over and saw it all."

To Al Gentry, the sheriff, the gambler's explanation was completely satisfactory; yes, there had been a slight grudge between the two, but it had been a fair fight. That was all the sheriff wanted to know.

It was not all there was to it for William. The cowboy did not regain consciousness until the following day. When he did, he was moved to the hotel. He left town soon after that and was never seen in Clarendon again, and the episode was quickly forgotten by all but William's parents and himself.

During the long hours of the day and night while William lived with the fear that his blow might prove fatal, he took stock of himself. Had he been wearing his gun, he would doubtless have used it in the blind rage that had possessed him. Had he done so—no matter with what excuse, instinctive urge for self-preservation or preservation of his self-respect—it was probable that he would have taken the life of another man or lost his own. He must make sure that he would never again be placed in so perilous a position.

When news came of the cowboy's recovery, William went to his room, washed his face, and combed his hair for the first time in twenty-four hours. After that, he went down into the store again to look for a container of the right size; when he found it, he put the revolver together and placed it in the wooden box.

He walked quickly to his parents' home, sought out his mother who was busy with dinner, and handed the box to her.

"Mother," he said, "this used to be my most prized possession. Until now, I didn't realize how easily it could have wrecked my life. Please put it away for a keepsake. I'm never going to wear it again. A fellow with my temper shouldn't have a gun within easy reach."

His mother made no reply, but that night after supper his father said, "Your mother told me about the gun; and it looks to us as if our boy has suddenly become a man."

About a month later B. H. White and Company was robbed. Early the next morning Rosie came into the store and said, "I almost lost my life last night—and much damage was done generally; in spite of which the robbery makes such a funny story that I myself want to tell it to you exactly as it happened.

"About a week ago Al Gentry came to me to tell me that overcoats and various things were being stolen all the time and he and his assistants were making a desperate effort to locate the gang doing these particular jobs. He said he had heard that the gang was planning a big haul from the Wood and Dickson Company and the Wells-Fargo Express, but he had been unable to discover the exact time. As you know, my store is across the tracks and more or less apart from the rest of the town. A few days later Gentry came to tell me again—this time to tell me that he had heard the robbers had decided the first two places too risky and had decided on me as the victim instead. Also, I was country treasurer and they thought might have a lot of money in the safe. That was true, but what they did not know was that the safe was very fine and large and contained inside it a burglar-proof chest in which I kept the money. The knob could be turned at only one place—otherwise it fell.

"Last night was to be the night of the robbery and Gentry asked me to cooperate in catching the robbers. The bookkeeper in the store often worked at night alone, using only one light—the large bright one over his desk—and we usually left the doors open to accommodate a late customer. There was a little railing around the office. Gentry requested that we have everything as usual that night except for the fact that I was to take the bookkeeper's place. I was a little dubious about this but consented nevertheless. He assured me he had everything arranged so there would be little risk; he, himself, would be hidden inside with a posse on the outside. I gave him the keys to the back and told him to make all the arrangements. That night I took my post as bookkeeper and if there were ever a scared person, I was that one. I was turning over the leaves of a ledger on the standing desk with the big light above me when the door opened and a man walked in. Most of the store was nearly dark, but even in the dimness I could see that he had a handkerchief over his face and was little more than a boy. He explained the handkerchief as he walked to me by saying he had neuralgia. He said he wanted a pair of twenty-five–cent socks, size 9½, and threw a crumpled five dollar bill in front of me. I gave him the socks, then turned toward the safe as I knew I did not have change for the bill in the small drawer. Of course, I had previously taken all the money out of the safe and put it in the burglar-proof chest, except a little scattered money in a drawer of the safe. I took out change for the bill and turned around—to find four pistols pointed at me. Three other men had come in quietly to join the first. It was so nearly dark I could not see their faces but heard plainly their order to throw up my hands. I complied asking what they wanted. 'The money in the safe,' they said. To which I replied, 'Well, gentlemen, there is nothing to prevent you from helping yourself.' 'We don't want any words out of you,' they answered. 'Just get under that light and keep your hands up.' I obeyed. One of them then crawled into the safe. I heard the knob fall and knew the cash was where they could not get it. Three of the men kept me covered, and the other began loading up with change from the small drawer, and also papers from the safe, which I suppose he thought would prove of value. Just then a shot came from the back of the store, where boxes were piled high with canned goods. I did not know it, but Gentry had hidden there, and the shot was to frighten the robbers. You can imagine my feeling. Another shot was fired, and I could see the pistols turned on me zig-zagging back and forth as if the men could not decide whether or not to shoot me. All the time I had a pistol under my cardigan, but luckily I kept cool. I now said, 'Boys, some one is shooting outside but you be careful how you handle your pistols because I am unarmed.' Although calm at the minute, I felt my life was not worth twenty-five cents. Just as I spoke, the sheriff came out from hiding with a pistol in each hand. Shots began to blaze around my head, clothing began to fall, canned goods to sputter and fall. I jerked out my gun and edged toward the man in the safe. When I reached him, I grabbed his coat, but it was only tied around his neck and he quickly slipped out of it. The sheriff was running toward the other three, who were trying to get out the front door. The man I was after ran through the little gate out of the office and down the aisle right behind the sheriff. I ordered him to halt but was afraid to shoot for fear of wounding Gentry. But the second Gentry went through the door, I blazed forth. One shot went through the front window but the other through the boy's shoulder. Again I ordered him to halt, but he continued running so I fired again, this time into the groin. He stumbled through the door and fell at the feet of the sheriff, who continued to shoot over him.

'I have broken my arm,' he said, and he had as he fell. They brought him in and laid him on a counter.

"The joke of it was that he was the first thing I had ever shot at and hit. I don't think I was even trying to hit him—just to scare him."

At the trial the prosecuting attorney decided that the robber was a novice who had fallen into bad company and asked Rosie not to stress an attempt had been made on his life. As a result, the young man was not prosecuted for murder but for robbery and received a sentence of only five years. The robbery made a great impression on William, and he decided that even though he had a temper and would not always wear a gun, it would be wiser to have a gun within reach. So once again, his gun went back to the store.

CHAPTER XXXII

The robbery was followed by rain, and suddenly it was spring. The winter had been a momentous one for Clarendon, with the town emerging from a mere huddle of tents into a promising trade center. An influx of settlers, many of them farmers, followed the coming of the railroad.

The tents were fast being replaced by substantial frame buildings. The most pretentious was the new Cain Hotel with a fine bannistered upstairs veranda and a huge dining room and bar. It occupied the corner by the railroad track. Next to it was Borscher's Saloon. A small dry goods store had been built on the empty lot between the saloon and Ralph's building. After that came an empty lot and, at the other end of the block, Stocking's Drugstore. Across the street were two more saloons, a rooming house, a candy shop, a bakery, and a butcher shop. A tent on the empty lot next to Stocking's Drugstore was the only tent. In it a Southerner with strong Democratic leanings had a small but, since it was the only one in town, lucrative insurance business. The first public school had opened after New Year's. Construction was well underway on the courthouse, and the Southern Methodists had laid the cornerstone for the town's first church. William was sorry to learn that his friend, the Reverend Mr.

Cooper, would never occupy the pulpit of the imposing structure. Being a Northern, not a Southern, Methodist, he was to be assigned to a district not under the control of the rival denomination.

There was also the prospect of the town's getting a federal post office building. William's father, who in reality had been acting postmaster for many months and who knew that Ralph was no longer interested in the job, was hoping to be appointed permanently after the coming presidential election. He was not counting on it, however, because he was a Yankee and a Republican, whereas most Texans, having come from the South, were Democrats.

William returned to the ranch in June to work until late fall, and the other members of the family settled into a very pleasant routine.

Suddenly it was Christmas and the New Year of 1889 began.

During the preceding three years there had followed a succession of events, although seemingly unrelated to the interests of the family, that were destined to play a major role in the success or failure of the Half Circle K. In 1885 John Adair died in St. Louis, leaving his estate to his widow, Cornelia Adair. By the time the estate was settled, Goodnight had been persuaded to accept as his one-third portion of the J. A. Ranch, a 140,000-acre tract lying below Red River and known generally as the Quitaque Ranch. He moved immediately away from his long-time home at headquarters to a location on the Fort Worth and Denver Railroad. Whether by intent or chance, his new home was not too far distant from the headquarters of the Half Circle K Ranch.

As the settlers increased in number, the antagonism between cattleman and farmer became intensified, especially when the colonization-minded state legislature began to support the farmers' efforts to wrest the grasslands from the cattle operators.

During the prelude to the struggle, when a few settlers had tried to claim free range, as well as during the real struggle, Goodnight was the champion of the concept that the range was for the stockman alone. He built the first barbed-wire fences. Because of the huge extent of his ranch, he probably enclosed more state land without the payment of lease money than any other single Panhandle cattleman. During the Clarendon trial under Judge Willis, he was the most frequently cited offender. But as William had already discovered, Goodnight was not only a formidable opponent on occasion but also a shrewd old frontiersman; not only an uncompromising individualist with no interest in the region except insofar as its development served his advancement, but also a realist, who recognized the trend of the times and saw that change was inevitable. With other cattlemen, he foresaw what later years were to prove: that a land, even though fertile, but low in rainfall, short on streams, and subject to droughts was primarily a grazing country. At any rate, he was determined to run cattle on Panhandle grass for the duration of his life. If the methods previously employed were no longer feasible, he would accommodate himself to those that were; if a lease bill of some sort was inevitable, he would see to it that it was the kind of bill that was of a minimum detriment to him personally.

To accomplish his purpose, he attached to his ranks one of the shrewdest Texas politicians, Temple Houston, the brilliant, persuasive son of the general who won Texas' freedom from Mexico. Through the combined efforts of Goodnight and Temple Houston the Sales Act Amendment of 1887 was introduced. The act was acceptable to the nester as well as to Goodnight: to the nester because it forced payment for grazing the public domain; to Goodnight because it reduced the amount of the lease rate from seven cents to the original four cents per acre and made possible the leasing of any land not previously filed on for as long as five years.

Since Goodnight's money, as well as his political influence, was behind the bill, he was in close contact with the powers in Austin. Immediately upon passage of the bill, he was able to procure a lease that gave him control not only of the land adjacent to the Half Circle K but also of most of the free grass area between the ranch and the Canadian River. Apparently, he had no scruples about doing so, although he knew that his friend Koogle's ranch was not large enough to handle its steer herd without this extra range and that the loss of it would create an all but insurmountable problem for the owners of the Half Circle K.

At the same time, Goodnight realized—as William pieced out Goodnight's thinking later—that the range was not of much value to him without the living waters inside the Half Circle K fence. To obtain the ranch was not going to be too difficult, for Goodnight obviously knew that payments on the Brush notes were a little in arrears, a fact that would make it easy to persuade the banker in Iowa to foreclose if he found a purchaser with cash.

Because Goodnight had other problems on his mind at the time, he was in no hurry to make a move, but when the day came on which the ranch was vital to his needs, he was prepared to do whatever was necessary to acquire it. His strategy was a shrewd one and spelled the doom both of the era of free grass in the Panhandle and of the Half Circle K. All Goodnight had to do was bide his time. Of the implication of all of this, William and his father were both unaware. They were conscious both of Goodnight's ruthlessness and of the passage of the new lease bill, but since previous bills had failed to alter the usage of free grass, they gave little concern to the latest one.

As far as they knew the outlook for the ranch was fairly good. After plentiful spring rains, the plains were carpeted with thick lush grass, there had been a good calf crop, and cattle prices were slowly rising. Both William and his father worked happily at their daily tasks. Clarendon continued to grow, with one notable addition. In the place where the tents of Feather Hill had originally stood, there was now a saloon and a so-called dance hall. It amused William as he made his grocery deliveries to the houses on the sand hills to notice how frequently a familiar cow pony of some cowboy he knew well could be found tied to the rail in front.

CHAPTER XXXIII

Besides the triple duty of helping his father to run both the grocery and dry goods store, as well as the post office, there was the problem with Ralph. Em was still in Washington. One drunken spree followed another. He remained sober only when locked in his room. At such times he often went half mad, fighting and threatening to kill his jailor—who generally was the boy. Ralph had been released from one of his enforced recovery periods for only a few days when the wedding of the Borscher girl was celebrated.

As the bride was the daughter of Clarendon's most prosperous saloon keeper and the groom an employee of the Fort Worth and Denver, everyone in town and everyone connected with the railroad was invited. In the absence of a church, the ceremony was performed in the largest room of the new schoolhouse. The reception was held a few blocks away at the Borscher home, which had been denuded of furniture to accommodate the crowd. A chef and his catering staff were brought up from Fort Worth to assure an elegant dinner. Unfortunately a blizzard struck two days before the wedding, and the wedding night was bitter. Deep snow covered the ground, making passage from school to house difficult and slow.

Once inside, however, the guests were soon unmindful of the inconvenience of getting there. Such a celebration as this had never before been seen in the Panhandle. The wine was the finest available, and, of more importance to a majority of the men present, it was plentiful.

Because of the inclement weather, his mother and Katie remained at home, and only William and his father attended the reception. As the evening progressed, the party grew more boisterous and unruly. William's father was planning to take his leave when a familiar voice from one of the back rooms caught his attention. There was Ralph in the adjoining room, the center of a group of young, local sports who were always ready to laugh at his jokes, to applaud his naughty French songs, and to drink with him at his expense. As William's father stepped into the door opening, he was greeted with peals of laughter. Ralph was just finishing an impersonation of some local figure, a performance at which he excelled.

Both embarrassed and fearful of the outcome, William and his father made a hasty retreat home. After several unusually hard days Ralph recovered. What his thoughts had been during this period no one ever discovered. On his first day of freedom, he packed his suitcase, walked to the station, and took the train for Washington. There were no words of explanation and none of apology. All connections with Texas were permanently severed.

Soon after Ralph's departure William's father began construction on the family cottage, which he hoped to have finished by fall. There would be a living room, dining room and three bedrooms; also a kitchen, which had been added to the rent house. Although there was a room for William, he did not plan to move. He preferred to stay in the room with the gambler because he was constantly needed in the store when in town and because he enjoyed being the gambler's roommate. Also the time to leave for the ranch was close at hand, so it was hardly worthwhile to make a change.

On William's return home in the late fall, he was able to give his father an encouraging report. The range had recovered well from the long drought; as a result, the steers, which were already in Chicago with Koogle, should bring a good price. If they did, the ranch would be able to make at least a token payment to Brush, after making the annual payment on the note for the cattle to Tandy.

Since Ralph's departure, Koogle had become the family's chief source of worry, and it made William's father particularly uneasy for Koogle to be in a large city alone. William knew that his father would have sent him along with Koogle had he been able to think of a good excuse. They both realized, however, that any change from the routine of previous years would make Bill suspicious and resentful. There was nothing to do but to sit and wait for the inevitable outcome. At last, after two weeks had gone by without any word from Bill, William's father reluctantly prepared to leave for Chicago on the next train.

But that very afternoon, shortly before closing time, Goodnight came into the store. Although his manner was hearty and jovial, neither William's father nor William was deceived. They were, nevertheless, totally unprepared for all they were to learn during the next half hour.

After a few pleasantries, the old man said, "I have come to make you an offer on the Half Circle K. I happen to know you still owe a lot on it. I have the money and will pay you a good price. What is your answer?"

Paying no attention to Goodnight's allusion to the financial straits of the company, William's father said, "The idea of selling the ranch has never been considered. I, for one, would be opposed to it."

"I was afraid you might take that position," Goodnight replied, "and mainly because you don't know all that has happened. I feel certain it will not take you long to come to my way of thinking when you learn the facts. To begin with, you no longer have partners to work with you. One has been in Washington for several months and the other is, by now, on his way to Mexico."

As Goodnight continued his distressing account, William and his father learned that Bill had reached Chicago on schedule and had received a good price for the cattle, as everyone expected. Unfortunately, after having the money for the cattle in hand, he obeyed one of those sudden impulses that had largely controlled his life; on the way to the train, he decided to take one drink to celebrate. One drink was followed by another, the beginning of a protracted drinking and gambling bout. It was only by chance that an employee of the stockyards happened upon him a week later in a dive in the Chicago slums. By that time Koogle was ill and penniless. Because Goodnight was known to be from the same town as Koogle, he was notified. He immediately wired instructions to get Koogle out of the country as quickly as possible at his expense.

"I telegraphed John Clay and Company to put him on the train for Mexico. I have a silver mine way up in the Chihuahua Mountains. There's not a saloon or a gambling hall within a hundred miles. Maybe he'll be able to pull himself together there. Who knows?"

Finding none of his arguments so far effective in persuading William's father to sell the ranch, Goodnight finally brought out the fact that he had leased the main pasture, the free grass area, of the Half Circle K behind the backs of his so-called friends. He made no explanation, and it was clear to William that, being the kind of man he was, he did not think one called for. According to his way of thinking, any other good businessman, placed in a similar position, would have done exactly as he did.

"Since dividing the property with the widow of my former partner, my third of the J.A. holdings is much too small for the number of cattle I plan to run. The Quitaque property is toward the south, but I like this plains country so much that I plan to continue living here and because of that it was to my advantage to get additional grassland as close to my new home as possible. The only way I could get hold of it was by law, so when the new lease law went into effect, I leased it."

As soon as Goodnight had gone, William and his father closed the store and hastened home to break the bad news to William's mother.

After giving the details of Goodnight's conversation, his father ended by saying, as if he alone were to blame, "I am so sorry, so very sorry for you and Katie and for Carrie and her babies. I should have been able to foresee all this long ago. It is no excuse, I know, but it is all incomprehensible to me. White told me recently that last year's interest had not been paid, but I did not worry too much about it for the steers were so fine and fat that I was confident about their bringing a good enough price to pay Brush up to date, and we had an option of renewal for two years. I had also heard rumors about the leasing of the open range, but I knew it was of no value to Goodnight without water, and our ranch controlled the water."

He was silent for a few moments, then added, "Can you understand a man who gives refuge to a troubled friend with one hand while he is taking the friend's ranch with the other? As for Bill—"

"Please don't say anything more," William's mother interrupted. "My poor dear brother, what will become of him now?"[1]

"You are right, and I shall make an effort not to blame him for his actions. We must face the fact, however, that everything is gone. All we'll have left is our home, and a little something is still due on that. As far as the ranch is concerned, Brush will be in by the end of the week, and when Corrigan hears about Bill, he'll probably come too, and he has the right. He not only owns half of that steer herd, but he will want to know what is to become of Carrie."

Both Corrigan and Brush acted quickly. Within a week Corrigan had come to Clarendon to move Carrie and her children home. How-

---

[1] Koogle's actions brought no change in the family's feelings for him. When his health failed he returned to Clarendon, where his sister gave him a home and loving care until he died.

ever, he made no mention of the cattle. The Iowa banker informed them that he would institute foreclosure proceedings at once unless the deal with Goodnight was consummated. To lose the ranch under these circumstances was a severe blow to both William and his father. Although the Half Circle K was a relatively small ranch, the abundance of water on it made it a choice piece of land with a value far in excess of the price Goodnight was offering.

There was nothing, however, to be done, with the banker and Goodnight in collusion, each working for his personal interest: the banker, to collect his loan in full and without delay, and Goodnight, to strike the shrewdest bargain possible. The only alternative was bankruptcy, and William's father refused even to consider such a suggestion. His partners were gone; he alone was responsible for the Half Circle K, and he refused to solve the problems of the ranch by throwing its losses into the laps of his creditors. Furthermore, he and William were hopeful of saving something from the wreckage. Goodnight did not want the steer herd, containing some three thousand head, which had been a separate venture to which Koogle had committed the Half Circle K partnership and which was mortgaged to Tandy, who preferred collecting the high rate of interest on his mortgage to enforcing liquidation, which so far he did not consider necessary. Only the land and the breeding herd had been involved in the Brush loan, and that was all Goodnight had been willing to buy to gain title to the ranch. That left William's family with the steer herd to fatten and sell in order to pay off the other debts of the partnership.

The chief problem was where to graze the cattle, now that they no longer had the ranch and the free grass to the west. Besides the Half Circle K steer herd, there was the herd belonging to Corrigan and Bill Koogle, which was being pastured on contract along with the Spur cattle. As for the Spur cattle, that was easy enough; they would be returned to South Texas.

The great difficulty, and one they discovered too late, was that within a few days after the passage of the new lease law, every bit of grazing land within easy distance of Clarendon had been placed under lease. Goodnight had seen to that. The only unfenced and unleased grass available was an area not far from Carson City. It was forty miles away and on the high plains. The job of moving the cattle had to be undertaken as soon as possible.

CHAPTER XXXIV

There were other complications in turning over the ranch to Goodnight. There had been several other brands, besides the Half Circle K, in what was considered the breeding herd. The Sugg cows, which the Half Circle K partners had gotten from Sugg when they bought his ranch, were marked with a Bar O; the cows that came with the Tandy-mortgaged steers with a Bar T; some seventy-five cows belonging to William and Bernie with a Flying W; and a bunch of mavericks owned by Red and a cowboy from the Turkey Tracks, with a Block Bar. The few hundred Tandy cows with the same brand as the steers would be cut out and put with the three thousand steers. As for William's and Bernie's cows, Goodnight offered to pay twelve dollars a head for them, and because it was a good price, they were glad to sell. Red's mavericks, however, were another matter. A maverick herd was always suspect since maverick collecting was the simplest way to steal cattle. What with the custom of branding every calf that was gathered with the brand of the cow it followed, the practice of letting some of the calves slip out of the herd to be branded later with a maverick brand was engaged in by many cowboys. Koogle had long suspected that this was the way Red kept increasing his little herd but had disregarded the matter because of his foreman's value as a top hand. Goodnight, being more businesslike, felt it unwise to have such a herd in the country. After much dickering with Red, he offered to buy the herd at twenty dollars a head, provided Red signed a contract in which he agreed not to start another maverick herd. Since the price was twice that of the market price of cows, the trade was thoroughly agreeable to Red.

Even though a shrewd operator, Goodnight, like all the other free grass cattlemen, was often careless in minor matters; and this was such an occasion. Going on the theory that no cowhand, even the foreman of an outfit, would own more than fifty or seventy-five head, Goodnight was willing to pay the high price in order to accomplish his purpose. As he turned away from Red, he caught sight of William standing with a group of cowboys, and the thought evidently occurred to him that if he could sell the herd to William, the cattle would be trailed to the new range along with the Half Circle K cattle, thus relieving him of the trouble of rebranding and shipping them out.

He came up to William and said, "I thought, maybe, you might like to take these mavericks off my hands. If so, make me an offer."

William stood silent for a minute. Like many other natural-born cowmen, he was blessed with a gift for which there is no explanation, the ability to remember each cow and calf as an individual animal, with its own distinguishing features, much as he would remember a human being. As a result, he was familiar with every animal on the ranch; he knew what brand it carried, in which pasture it belonged, and where he had seen it last. Since to his knowledge there were about two hundred Block Bars in the herd for which Goodnight was going to pay twenty dollars a head, he did not feel himself in a position to make an offer.

"I am sorry, sir," he said, "I would love to have them but, even with our savings and what you are paying us for the cattle, Bernie and I don't have more than eleven hundred dollars between us."

"Then eleven hundred it is," Goodnight said, all joviality. "Just get them out of the country, along with the others." And the deal was closed.

Meanwhile the lawyers were busy drawing up the papers for the sale of the ranch. In checking the abstracts, one of them discovered that the Allen Creek land was not part of the ranch, and that William and his cousin Bernie had filed on it. Goodnight promptly sent for William. There was no joviality this time; he demanded that William make a quitclaim deed over to him immediately.

"Why should we do that? Bernie and I have homesteaded the land, and it belongs to us exactly as it would to any other settler who had done the same thing."

"Because both Brush and your uncle told me it was part of the Half Circle K," Goodnight roared.

"Well, if they told you that," William said, "they told you something that wasn't so, and I'm not responsible for that. In the beginning, my uncle did suggest that I file on that land, but I thought I was too young. When I did file, I wasn't thinking about the ranch, and neither Brush nor my uncle knew anything about it. Anyway, you know and I know that the same law that helped you take our pasture away from us forbids any person's turning his claim over to the outfit he works for. I couldn't have let the ranch have our four sections on Allen Creek if I had wanted to. They would have had to buy it to get it, and if you want it, you'll have to buy it too."

Clamping his lips, Goodnight then made what he called an offer.

When he heard it, William shook his head.

"All you seem to want to do is to reimburse us for what we've paid the state. You forget that we've put in a lot of time and work on the place. We've not only slept there, but we've broken part of the land."

Seasoned and vastly experienced old trader that he was, Goodnight was not able to keep his usually poker-faced expression from giving away something of all that was going on in his mind. With so much at stake, William was watching him intently. For a moment the old cowman was complacent, even patronizing. The next moment the smugness went out of his opponent's face. Possibly, William thought, Goodnight has remembered that he himself is not too well liked, that general sentiment is in favor of the settler, against the large landholder, and that by arousing a controversy he might lose the Allen Creek sections altogether.

It became clear that in these split seconds Goodnight had come to a decision. He was not going to try force; he was going to buy. All the same, he clung to his original intention of not paying the boys direct profit on the land. It must be sold him for exactly its original cost—a whim that, as nearly as William could figure it, was prompted solely by Goodnight's wanting the appearance of getting his own way.

"I'll reimburse you for your work all right, but in other ways. Sell me the land for your payments, and I'll buy back from you the Block

Bars that I sold and give you fifteen dollars a head for them. Besides that, I'll add a three-dollars-a-head bonus on your own herd of cattle. That satisfy you?"

William's first reaction was an odd sense of annoyance born of sheer puzzlement. There must be a catch somewhere. As closely as he could figure it, in the short time he had to reply, the deal would net him and Bernie a clear profit of three thousand dollars. Red's cattle were at best worth ten dollars a head. Why would a shrewd old frontiersman like Goodnight have paid Red twice their value, only to turn around and sell them for a fourth of what he had paid for them, and now offer to buy them back at fifteen dollars a head? It did not make sense!

And then, suddenly, the truth dawned on him. There was only one possible explanation: Goodnight had no idea of the actual size of Red's herd! William hastily closed the deal.

Red's cattle were not out on the plains, but in a nearby pasture where they could be gathered and branded with ease. William had already made up his mind to act as fast as he and Bernie were able, before the old man discovered his mistake. William could already hear Goodnight's roar when the old man realized that he had allowed himself to be outsmarted by a mere boy, and William took a grim satisfaction in evening the score, even a little, with the person who had done such great harm to his family.

The Block Bar herd was branded and delivered. When Goodnight saw the size of it, he looked black but made no comment. He merely announced that he would be in the banking department of Wood and Dickson's the following morning to make payment.

They met there as agreed, and William received his check. He was about to leave the store when he noticed that the amount of the check was not adequate. He turned at once and went back to Goodnight.

Goodnight exploded, "What the hell did you expect? There were twice as many Block Bars as I thought there was going to be. With all the money you made on them, you don't deserve a bonus on your own cattle; so you aren't getting it."

Firm in his intention not to be outdone by Goodnight, William shook his head. "What I deserve doesn't have anything to do with it. An agreement is an agreement. Bernie and I have kept our part of the bargain, and we expect you to keep yours. I hope you'll remember that we preferred all the time to sell our land outright. It was your idea to do it this roundabout way, and it was just our good luck that it turned out so well for us."

"God damn it, you knew all the time how many Block Bars there were."

"Certainly, I knew," William said calmly, "and I would have told you if you'd asked me; but you didn't, and I didn't think it would be to my advantage to volunteer the information, any more than you felt it was to yours to tell my family that you were leasing their grass out from under them."

The reference to the lease increased the old man's fury. He shook his fist in William's face and shouted, "You'll never get that extra money."

William's anger had mounted steadily. He tore the check into shreds and threw it on the table in front of Goodnight.

"You aren't too popular in these parts, and I have a lot of friends, the kind that not only carry six-shooters but know how to use them. If we aren't paid by tomorrow, I'll get out an injunction against you. If that doesn't work, my friends and I are going after our cattle, and I don't believe there's a single boy in your outfit who'll try to stop us."

He did not wait for an answer, but turned on his heels and walked out. Cook, the banking clerk, who had been an uncomfortable witness to the whole exchange, came after him. As William got on his horse, Cook caught the bridle.

"Go back," Cook pleaded, "and apologize. Don't forget he's the biggest man in the Panhandle. He'll never forgive you for what you just did, and he can ruin the chances for a good boy like you. He won't hesitate to do it, either; he doesn't like for anybody to get in his way."

William refused to listen. He had learned from his experiences with Red that survival in the West depended as much on inner courage as on physical bravery and stamina. The enemy must be met face to face without fear, regardless of consequences. He knew perfectly well that Goodnight had the power to destroy anyone, but he also knew that he was not afraid of the old man, and the time to let him know it was the present.

William did not gloat over his triumph, but there was satisfaction in finding that his assessment of his powerful antagonist's character had been correct. A check for the full amount was in William's letter box the following morning, and there was no more trouble over the Block Bar herd deal.

CHAPTER XXXV

With his personal affairs in order, William hastened to join the Half Circle K outfit, which was busy rounding in preparation for moving the cattle off Goodnight's land and onto the new pasture as quickly as possible. Since William was now in charge, it was up to him to make the decisions, and he had decided to put their cattle on the free grass land to the north of their former ranch headquarters. It was country that lay on the high plains and was unfenced, but both grass and water on it were plentiful. The outfit had to get started. Fall was already drawing to a close, and winter could clamp down any day.

The work progressed slowly because the outfit had dwindled to a few hands. The majority of the boys had left as soon as they heard about the sale of the ranch; others had stayed on only long enough to gather the cattle. Red[1] had gone back to his former boss in the Territory. By the time William started the cattle to their new pasture, faithful Art Sherrod was his only assistant. It was almost Christmas before they turned the cattle loose, and Art, who was to handle the herd through the winter, was settled in an old log cabin built years before for the line riders. William returned to town.

On his first morning in Clarendon, Cook, the banking clerk, stopped him as he rode down the street past Wood and Dickson's to ask him to come into the store. Goodnight wanted to see him. A little

---

[1] When Red died of cancer many years later, it was William who paid his hospital bills.

hesitantly, William tied his horse and prepared to obey the summons of the man he so heartily disliked. Ever since their argument over the deal, he had felt that it would be wise to stay out of his recent adversary's way as much as possible. He had to admit to himself, however, that curiosity as well as courtesy prompted him to follow the Wood and Dickson banker into his office.

Once again, Goodnight took William by surprise. The unpredictability of the cattle baron with his reputation for ruthlessness continued to bewilder William; like the Texas winds, without forewarning, he blew hot one day and cold the next. William found himself greeted, not with the rancorous condescension he had expected, but with the warmth and friendliness of an intimate family friend.

Without the least allusion to the last time they had met, and without any preliminary, Goodnight said, "My wife, who is very fond of your ma, thinks schooling is the most important thing a boy can get. She and I don't always agree, but in the end she usually gets her way. We've both been watching you ever since the time you visited at the ranch. She has one thing in mind for you, and I have another. After a lot of talking, we've hit on a plan that may serve both our ends. Mollie wants to send you East to school for two years; then, when you come home, you're to have a job on the ranch. I'll keep you right with me, so as soon as you know all the ropes, you can take over for me. I'm gettin' to be an old man, and I think you have the makings of a fine cattleman. How does all that sound to you?"

There was not much time to think. Any hesitation in answering would amount to a lack of appreciation of what was unquestionably a very generous offer on the part of Goodnight and his wife, but William did not need any time.

"It's hard for me to answer you, sir," he said, "and I hope you won't think that I don't appreciate what you are offering me, but I can't accept. I'm a little over nineteen. I don't have time to stop work for two years. Besides, I don't believe you have to be educated to become a successful cattleman, and that's what I'm going to be."

Again, Goodnight surprised him. Far from taking umbrage at his refusal, the old man responded with a pleased grin and a hearty slap on his shoulder, "I knew you were a smart kid. You're sure right. You don't need books to learn how to run cattle. I've been telling Mollie that right along."

It was the end of the interview. They parted, this time pleased with each other. Only William's father and mother were disappointed when he told them about Goodnight's offer.

"An education isn't just a tool with which to earn a superior livelihood, William," his father said slowly. That was all either of his parents said, but the sad look on his mother's face spoke loudly enough, and he could almost read his father's mind. It was as if his father was reproaching himself for having brought him West and was asking himself: what is this West doing to my son, to blind him to the enrichment that comes into a life from learning the mistakes of the past?

CHAPTER XXXVI

The first blizzard of 1890 struck in mid-January. On the same day, a wire came from Corrigan with instructions to gather the partnership steers for immediate shipment to feed lots in Kansas. It was a peremptory and unreasonable order, which William opposed. In the first place, he resented the air of authority assumed by Corrigan after Koogle's departure for Mexico. William felt that Corrigan had no legal claim on the ranch other than the agreement to pasture the steers he owned with Koogle. By this agreement, the ranch had the obligation to work and graze his herd along with the ranch cattle. During the sunny and warm time when the ranch was turned over to Goodnight, it would have been a simple operation to cut out the steers and trail them to a shipping point, as had been done with the Spur herd. But Corrigan had chosen not to do that. Instead, he had waited until the cattle were scattered over the plains, the winter was bitter, and the Half Circle K outfit was disbanded. It looked as if he were intentionally attempting to punish everyone connected in business or otherwise with Koogle.

William's father, however, viewed the matter differently. Being humiliated that a member of his family had brought disgrace and hardship to a woman of Carrie's kind, he felt morally bound to abide by any decision Corrigan might make. Furthermore, he was grateful for Corrigan's having given the deserted wife a home and for his continued care of her. William, too, felt sympathy for Carrie, but he could not understand his father's sense of obligation to her. Apparently, his father was not taking into account the fact that it was Carrie's husband who had misappropriated ranch funds and brought about the loss of the ranch.

Finally, on seeing that his father was deaf to argument, William set about assembling an emergency outfit. Many of the Half Circle K boys were still in town and without jobs, but they showed no inclination to undergo the hardship of a winter drive or to accommodate a former employer who no longer owned a ranch. When Corrigan was notified that no one would undertake a job without a bonus, he agreed to the bonus but added the stipulation that no former ranch hand be hired and that William be put in charge. William obeyed Corrigan's instructions with one exception; he took Art along as straw-boss.

William soon succeeded in getting together a sufficient number of men and horses and the work of gathering the cattle began.

Carson City, which was to be the shipping point, was not too far from the Half Circle K's free grass range, and that was an advantage. The major problem arose from the fact that the cattle were not only scattered but scattered over the plains where the thermometer stayed around zero. Every lake and water hole was frozen over. Before the cattle were able to drink, a thick crust of ice had to be chopped through. The cattle never bedded down but milled constantly throughout the night, making it necessary for the men to stand guard to keep the cattle from scattering. It was so cold that it was impossible for a man to stay in the saddle for more than thirty minutes without danger of freezing. As a result, they took turns riding around the herd and, after tying their horses to the wagon, warming at the fire.

By the end of the third day, all of them were nearing the point of exhaustion, and the herd amounted to more than a thousand head. At that point, William saw that something had to be done. They were working to the north of the Half Circle K headquarters. Not far distant was the line riders' log cabin; near the cabin was a huge corral. About four miles farther on, the old Half Circle K drift fence ran into the Salt Forks forming a corner. In order to give as much relief as possible to the men and to facilitate a job that had turned out to be even more difficult than was feared at the start, William moved the outfit and herd to the cabin. Once there, he gave orders to stop the wagon and crowd the cattle into the corral. By doing this, he would at least be able to provide his men with a few hours of sleep. His plan was to cover a ten-mile radius out from camp on the following day. Only the cook, Art, who was to act as straw-boss, and William himself were to remain behind—the cook, to prepare a hot dinner, and he and Art to drive the steers that had already been gathered into the corner where the drift fence and the creek, serving as natural barriers, would make it possible for the two men to hold them. As each of the other men returned with his cattle, he was to throw them into the big herd; after that, he would go back to camp to eat and to get a change of mount.

The boys who were to do the gathering were up and off on schedule the next day, but it was well into the morning before William and Art were able to get the cattle into the corner. The temperature had not risen by one degree, and it was beginning to snow. Although they built several fires—a safe distance away from the cattle—the steers were milling so badly that neither William nor Art could dismount for long enough to get warm. By noon their horses were tiring rapidly. With their pool of horses all the way back at the camp, there was no way to procure a fresh mount without riding four miles. There had been no sign of any of the other boys. As the afternoon wore on, William realized that he and his partner would soon be afoot, and he sent Art back to get new mounts.

An hour dragged by, then another, and another, with his anxious eyes catching no sight of either Art or any of the others in the grey light; meanwhile, William had the desperate job of holding the restless herd in the corner without help. It was almost night when Art finally came into view, on foot, leading old Bullet, one of the horses from Fred Patchin's former string and the meanest animal on the ranch. Bullet pitched with or without provocation. Unfortunately, he was the only pony Art had been able to catch. Although Art was an excellent hand with horses, his sensible fear of being thrown and, if badly injured, freezing to death before help reached him in the storm had made him walk all the way from camp. With the refractory Bullet to lead, he had found the return trip difficult and slow.

A fresh horse for one of them was a necessity. Being the better bronc buster of the two, William led old Bullet to the creek where the sand was soft and, after having his stirrups tied, let Bullet pitch himself out. After Bullet got tired enough, he submitted quietly to being ridden until relief finally came.

The story the other cowboys told when they came riding in was that the morning's rounding had gone without difficulty, but on the drive back to camp, the cattle became unmanageable. The steers wanted to drift ahead of the storm, which was blowing in the wrong direction. By the time they reached camp, each with his individual bunch, the horses were too exhausted to push on for another four miles. It was only after picking up fresh mounts at the cabin, that the riders were able to get the cattle to the corner.

When William and Art finally returned to the cabin, they had been without food and in the saddle for twenty straight hours. The next day they drove the herd on toward Carson City.

On reaching town, William found a telegram from Corrigan, instructing him not to send the cattle to feed lots in Kansas City, but to take them instead to Chicago to be sold on the open market. It meant another week of hard work and little sleep for him if he were to see the job through to the end, as he was determined to do. Without a word of complaint against the owner of the steers, he followed instructions. As soon as the loading was finished, he paid off the men and climbed on the train with the cattle.

It was William's first experience in taking cattle to market. As boss of the train, it was his responsibility to keep the steers on their feet at all times; once down in a crowded cattle car, an animal was easily trampled to death. At regular intervals throughout the day and night, he worked his way from one end of the train to the other, prodding into a standing position any steer that showed an inclination to lie down. Attached to the end of the train was a small caboose with a stove and chairs, but with no bunks; sleep was a luxury to be indulged in, even on long runs like this, only in the intervals when the cattle were unloaded and herded into pens, where they were watered and fed, or while the cars were sidetracked in Chicago to await being hauled into the yards.

As the result of his good care, the steers reached the yards in fine shape. Being fat and heavy four and five year-olds, they brought the unusually good price of $2.10 per hundredweight. Corrigan declared himself satisfied with the shipping and the deal; he even added a bonus to William's wages as well as to the wages of the other cowboys.

William reached home with frostbitten fingers and toes, and with the determination never to own anything but cows and never to graze them anywhere but on the prairies below the high plains. After he had rested, he was well satisfied with himself: Corrigan's commission had been successfully carried out, and he had earned his first wages as a professional cowboy in charge of a herd and in the employ of someone outside his own family.

CHAPTER XXXVII

The grim experience of gathering and taking Corrigan's steers to market proved to be a prelude to the following year, which was destined to be a mixture of hard work, frustration, failure, and success. To begin with, William was far from being in accord with his father about the older man's responsibility for the ranch's entire indebtedness. As he saw it, his uncle's irresponsibility, the blizzard of 1886, the drought, and market fluctuations were matters over which no one individual had control; it seemed, therefore, not reasonable to him that one man, his father, should pay for the lack of knowledge of three and the follies of two of the three. His father, however, remained adamant on the subject of his responsibility, and William's affection and respect for his father kept him from pressing his arguments. Although he received no wages for his work in the store or with the remnant herd, he continued.

On 22 January 1890, a few days after his return from Chicago, his sister Katie and Ben Chamberlain were married. Her trousseau was bought in Dallas. The wedding gown was of ivory satin trimmed in rose point lace. The service was performed in the recently completed Methodist Church by the Reverend W. A. Cooper.

Ever since relinquishing his herd and the Allen Creek pasture to Goodnight, William had been casting about for an equally good investment. He had difficulty finding one partly because he never considered any enterprise but cattle raising and largely because cattle raising called for land, and land was at a premium in the area below the cap rock. Every day brought new nesters to besiege the courts for assistance in securing school land for homesteading. The stockmen, loath to relinquish land, were equally determined to close all doors in the face of the intruders by means of the new lease laws. The few farmers who managed to acquire pieces of land found themselves surrounded by the extensive holdings of the big operators, to the great disadvantage of both. Antagonism between the two groups grew steadily. In the struggle that ensued, the cattlemen were victorious for the time being, at least.

Cattle were everywhere. They were a common sight even in town, for Jeffreys, the former owner of the Scab Eights, who had the Heart land under lease, watered many of his bunches at the lake just a mile beyond Clarendon and had to drive his cattle through the town to get there. He was able to do this by a provision of the lease laws, which gave every cattleman the right to graze sixty head of cattle on the public domain for every section he owned or leased. It was this provision that presented William the eagerly awaited opportunity to get back into the cattle business.

Through a friend he learned about three sections of Heart land that Jeffreys had refused to include in his lease because of their isolation from the main block of the ranch and their location a mile or so up the railroad track, where no water was available. The poor location made no difference to William, for like Jeffreys he had no use for the land as pasture. He wanted it merely as the legal means of turning cattle loose on the public domain near the lake.

For several weeks William had had his eye on a small but fine herd of heifers. He hurriedly made the lease and purchased the heifers. As soon as they were branded, he turned them loose near the lake.

Everything went well for several weeks, until one afternoon an R.O. cowboy who had once worked for the Half Circle K came into the store with disturbing news. On his way into town, he had noticed an unusual looking bunch of cattle in the R.O. pasture closest in. Having stopped to look at them more closely, he saw a wide variety of brands. The heifers, however, all bore William's Flying U Bar mark. The unfamiliar brands possibly belonged to townspeople and farmers. But why, he began to wonder, would cattle, which usually grazed on the outskirts of town, be in a fenced-in R.O. pasture ten miles out and all the way across the Salt Fork? Something must be wrong, he concluded, and William should be told at once.

"In an R.O. pasture?" William said after listening to the cowboy's recital. "How could my heifers get inside a fence, unless someone opened the gate and drove them in?"

"Not without help, that's a sure thing. If I was you, I'd ask old man Jeffreys. I'd do that before I did anything else. Ever since that old son-of-a-gun moved from Scab Eights and leased what's left of the Heart Ranch, he's got the notion everything belongs to him—all the land around the town and 'specially around the lake where the cattle water."

Jeffreys was a well-known old-timer who, like Goodnight, went by the customs and mores of the free grass era. William had never had any dealings with him but knew from Jeffreys' reputation that he was hard and tough and inclined to run roughshod over everything and everyone in his path. To round the cattle and throw them into another man's pasture was the kind of thing he would not hesitate to do if the cattle happened to graze land he felt to be his by right of occupancy. Whether he was guilty of the offense in this particular case, William did not know but he knew someone who would know.

Jeffreys had a cousin who for some reason was permitted to stay on his payroll although he never made more than a pretense of working. His main interests were drinking and telling all he knew about other people's business. There was nothing concerning Jeffreys and his affairs that he did not know. He could be found at almost any hour of the day or night at Borscher's Saloon, in the company of a cowboy of similar tastes. When William approached them, he found them in no condition to withstand the threats of a younger man who was not only angry but strong and steady on his feet. They readily admitted that it was they who had followed Jeffreys' instructions to get every cow but his own off the land around the lake.

From the saloon, William went directly to Jeffreys, who, as was to be expected, began by denying any knowledge of the whereabouts of the Flying U Bar cattle. However, he soon saw that William knew exactly what had transpired and that a change of tactics was necessary. Like Goodnight during the dispute over Red's maverick herd, Jeffreys changed his manner to a mixture of joviality and threat. But William was not impressed. Once again, he was certain of his rights and, being certain, had no intention of having them arbitrarily set aside by Jeffreys or anyone else.

"There are only two things you can do to satisfy me; you can either buy the heifers at a good profit for me, or you can return them. In either case, it'll be your men who will do the gathering."

Jeffreys, who was clearly still determined to rid the range around the lake of all but his own cattle, shook his head.

"I have a better idea. Leave your heifers where they are until the summer work starts, then you can tag along with the R.O. outfit and pick them up as you come to them. Meanwhile, they will be on fine grass, and I'll pay you your wages myself. Besides, I'll reimburse you for any loss in number."

It was very clear to William that Jeffreys was willing to go to any lengths to retain possession of the public domain around Clarendon and the lake. The idea of unlawfully using another man's range and of paying someone wages to be a party to it was anything but agreeable to William.

Disgusted, he said, "You may think it's all right to leave my cattle in an R.O. pasture without Mr. Rowe's knowledge and without payment, but that doesn't mean I like it. As for riding with the R.O. outfit this summer, I wouldn't have the time even if Mr. Rowe and the boys were willing, and besides, there aren't enough heifers in my bunch to be scattered all over the R.O. Ranch. No sir, your men know exactly where they are now, and since they put them there, they can go get them and bring them back to the place where they found them."

Without waiting for an answer, he turned and walked away, determined to ride out to R.O. headquarters the next day to explain to Alfred Rowe how Flying U Bar cattle came to be in one of his pastures.

The following morning, as he made ready for his trip to the ranch, he was given information that added serious complications to the whole business of the heifers. He had been aware for some time that cattle stealing on a major scale was increasing in the Panhandle. Around Tascosa and down in Collingsworth County, where the Rockingchairs was located and where the R.O. had a large leased pasture, there were organized gangs that often stole as many as fifty head at a time. They were proving to be a costly problem for both ranches. So far, however, the area around and to the north of Clarendon had been relatively free of thieves, and William had given little thought to the matter.

It happened that in the very center of the R.O.'s Collingsworth pasture were two sections owned by a tough character named Frey, who, together with four companions, constituted the most notorious of all the gangs, also the most successful one because of Frey's proximity to the Indian Territory, where beef brought high prices at the army posts. That morning just as he was about to set out for the R.O. Ranch headquarters, a Rockingchair hand told William that twenty-seven of his heifers were in Frey's pasture.

That Frey and his crowd were killers, William knew. He also knew that he had chosen to live in a rugged part of the country where fear alone was enough to bring about a man's defeat. To face Frey in his own bailiwick was going to call for all the courage and shrewdness he could muster. He did not hesitate. His herd was very small, but it was his and was all he had. He was not going to let any man take it from him without a fight even though there was a chance that a fight with Frey might cost his life.

He spent the night at the R.O. Ranch, as he had planned. The R.O. owner and he sat up until late discussing the problem of thieving, which in urgency was of equal importance to both of them. The next morning when William was saddling his horse, Rowe joined him again.

"I see you aren't wearing a gun," he said. "That's a foolish thing to do; you're going to be up against a gang of murderers. My advice to you is to take this Winchester. It has the R.O. brand on it. Go straight to Frey's house; the chances are he'll be there alone. I have heard that the others are off somewhere. If he is there, don't stop to explain. Kill him and get out with the cattle as fast as you can. When the case goes to trial, I'll get you a good lawyer, and we'll swear that you were working for me and were shooting in self-defense."

It all sounded very logical, but William was not misled. He sensed at once that it was not his but Rowe's own problem that Rowe was trying to solve; and William was surprised that a gentleman like Rowe would urge on another a course of action that he, himself, under no circumstances, would have considered following. It was very unsportsmanlike, to say the least.

However, it was not the question of motives but a decision made earlier in the day that made the acceptance of Rowe's proposal impossible. Still in practice on the frontier, was the unwritten law that a man never shot an adversary who was either unarmed or was standing with his back turned. According to William's calculations, his one and only chance to get on and then off Frey's land without being killed was to ride up to Frey unarmed. To make the absence of a gun on his person plainly visible, he wore only pants and a shirt. The coat, which would have been comfortable in the cool spring weather, was left behind. He did not bother to explain all this to Rowe. He simply thanked the Englishman for his kind offer and refused.

When he reached Frey's house, William found Frey's wife busy jerking beef from a freshly killed calf. Close by stood a heifer, bearing the Flying U Bar brand.

Before he had time to address Frey's wife, she said in a surly voice, "The old man ain't here. What's your business?"

"I've come for my cattle. Would you show me where the pasture is?"

Without stopping, she nodded toward the south. "Right through the gate. But you'd better not touch nothin'. He shore wouldn't like it."

"I'm sorry," William said, "but I won't have time to wait for him. I'm going ahead and get my heifers. Before I drive them off, I'll put them in the corral, so that you can see they all have my brand on them."

It was difficult to tell from her expression whether she was unaware that the cattle had been stolen or whether she knew and did not care. Since it mattered little either way, and since she showed no sign of having anything more to say, he hurried on about his business. His cattle were grazing not very far away; he gathered them quickly and drove them toward the house and into the corral for the old woman to inspect the brands. He was about to drive the last one in when he saw Frey ride up. Frey stopped short, without saying anything either to his wife or to William, carefully untied his Winchester and placed it across his saddle, ready to fire. Only then he demanded to know William's business on his land.

William answered Frey as he had answered the old woman.

"Goddam it," Frey said, "this brand belongs to a friend of mine in the Territory. I'm just keeping this little bunch for him."

William felt his anger boiling up in him. "That's a lie, and you know it. These are my cattle, and I don't intend to let anybody take them from me."

Frey sounded more menacing. "Young feller, if you knew me better, you'd have sense enough to know that nobody can get away with what you're trying to do and stay alive."

This was the time to make his point, and William realized it. "I know the kind of man you are, all right. However, before you let loose with your rifle, I want you to remember that I'm not wearing a gun—also, that I spent last nite at the R.O. headquarters. Mr. Rowe and the boys know where I went this morning, and why I'm here. If

I'm not back with my cattle by sundown, they're coming to find me. They also know I am unarmed, and, if they find me dead, they won't give you time to say a word; they'll be too busy stringing you up to that nice, tall cottonwood over there by the house."

It was clear to Frey that the logic of what William said was unanswerable. "By God, I've been outsmarted by a kid that's just been weaned. Take your damn heifers and get the hell out of here before I come to my senses and put a bullet square through that sassy mouth."

Then Frey dismounted and stamped into the house.

By midafternoon William and his cattle were back at R.O. headquarters. On the following morning, with the help of one of the R.O. boys, he located the few heifers that had been left in the R.O. pasture, threw them in with the ones he had recovered from Frey, and drove them back to the lake.

Jeffreys did not make good his promise to pay for any missing heifers; neither did he repeat his attempt to run the Flying U Bars off the public domain. That much had been gained—that, and still another lesson: a man who wanted to run cattle successfully had to own or to control fenced-in land with an ample water supply!

CHAPTER XXXVIII

On reaching home after the three days required to retrieve his cattle, William learned that his father had been notified of his permanent appointment as postmaster. In the letter from Washington, there was also the assurance that work on the post office building was scheduled for early spring. It was good news, and William regretted that his father received it with some misgivings. There had been another aspirant for the post office appointment, a young man who was the town's only insurance agent and a Democrat. During the months before the appointment was made official, this opponent often spoke harsh words over a Republican being permitted to serve even as the temporary postmaster. It was inconceivable to him, as he often stated, that anyone outside the right party had even been considered for a federal post in a community as solidly Democratic as Clarendon. William's father, with his usual equanimity and consideration for others, paid little attention to the rancor and the verbal attacks of his political opponent, even though anything that tended to create an unpleasant situation was distasteful to his gentle nature. William, on the other hand, resented the insurance man's continued tirade and demanded that their insurance policy on the store be placed with a Fort Worth agency.

His father would not hear of it. "Let's not be vindictive toward a man whose fault lies chiefly in wanting the position I was fortunate enough to get. There is not so much business of his kind anyway in a place this size, and I have no intention of depriving him of ours."

Because William quickly recognized his father's attitude toward his political opponent as only an expression of the goodness that lay deep within him, he had no desire to oppose him further. So the policy remained where it was, in the hands of a small and disgruntled man.

Spring was ripe with the promise of summer, and William was eager to work at anything that paid him well. Since he had earned a reputation for being steady, dependable, and an excellent hand at shipping horses and cattle, he had been able to make arrangements with several of the smaller operators to take their cattle to market in the fall. There was little that Art Sherrod could not handle alone at the ranch. Since he and William constituted the present Half Circle K outfit, William would have to help when rounding and branding time came, but that was not until midsummer. If he could persuade someone else to work temporarily in the store, he would be free for several months to work elsewhere. Bernie agreed.

As soon as Rowe heard that William was looking for something extra to do, Rowe offered him a job with the R.O. outfit. When William refused, Rowe suggested he become an "outside" man for the ranch and travel from ranch to ranch collecting any R.O. strays. William was delighted, for an outside man was always a top hand, who received extra wages, and a person of good character.

The methods of ranching had changed even in the few years since William's early days under Red with the Half Circle K outfit. The big roundup was no longer necessary, for the lease laws and fencing had put a stop to the drifting that had been inevitable during the open range days of the free grass era. It was chiefly cattle rustling that made the outside man important. Inasmuch as the ranches tried to work together, a schedule of rounding had been set up that made it possible for the outside man to travel a circuit from the roundup of one ranch to that of the next.

William was given the usual mount of eight horses and assigned to the southern area. He left for the first ranch a week after his twentieth birthday. William did not return to Clarendon until well into the summer. Nothing important happened in the course of his tour of duty, but his job was rich in the kind of learning that would stand him in good stead in the future. By the time he was finished, he had firmly imprinted the map of every ranch and of each of its pastures on his mind. He had also had a chance to study the traits and personality and to assess the integrity of each one of the numerous cowboys and of the ranch owners as well.

It would be necessary within a week or ten days for him to leave again, this time to round the Half Circle K cattle out from Carson City. One morning while William was working in the store, his new brother-in-law, Ben Chamberlain, came in.

"Lucky thing I ran into you. I've been waiting for you to get back to discuss some business with you. I have a proposition that may interest you. You may not remember, but some time before your sister and I were married, I filed on a section of land out from town. Why I filed I do not know for I'm no farmer and never had an idea of becoming one. Anyway, it's good land with a creek running through it, and I have it. It is a homestead claim and you and I both know that even if I wanted to live out there, your sister is never going to be happy except in the house with her mother. Because I have not been spending the required time out there, I have been expecting trouble over it. So far there has been none, maybe because we don't own the house we live in. The thought has come to me that by paying me what I have paid the state you might be willing to take the land off my hands. It would be a satisfactory deal for both of us."

It was the opportunity William had long waited for and feared might never come. To have land of his own again! He wanted that more than anything else. He was not forgetting, however, the fact that he was still not of age, and that the country surrounding Clarendon was not the isolated area that Allen Creek land had been. There was a good chance that he might run into trouble, but he was going to risk it.

They quickly reached an agreement. Ben would continue to do whatever was necessary until William returned from Carson City. By that time William's work with the remnant herd and the cattle shipments would be finished, and he would still have plenty of time to break ground, do some fencing, and sleep the required number of nights on his new homestead.

Having concluded the details of his deal with his brother-in-law, he began preparations to leave for Carson City. A makeshift outfit was again assembled, and soon the rounding, branding, and shipping was under way. The cattle, which had thrived during the summer, brought an unusually good price on the market. He returned home with the feeling that all the business connected with the Half Circle K could easily be finished by the next spring, and that the amount received for the cattle would not fall short of paying off the ranch's indebtedness.

He left again shortly to take a load of cattle to Chicago for some of the townspeople, as he had agreed to do. When he returned from Chicago, he hoped to be able to have a few quiet months in town. For a few days, he was permitted to enjoy the settled life; then, one afternoon a man came into the store with the message that Menasco wanted to see him. Realizing that his gambler friend would not send for him except on a matter of urgency, he hurried over to Borscher's Saloon.

"All this may not mean a thing," Menasco said, "but I thought I'd pass it on to you anyway. One of the Fort Worth and Denver engineers was in here last night, doing a lot of drinking. Among other things, he said he was going to move his wife into town in a few days to help him homestead one of the best places around Clarendon. When somebody asked him how he had managed to get a location when so many others had tried and failed, he said he knew someone in the right place; then he added that no kid should be allowed to take up land anyway. When he said that, I remembered that Ben had transferred his land to you. Afterwards, I inquired about the fellow. It seems his wife has a brother who is a clerk in the land office in Fort Worth."

William thanked Menasco but made no comment beyond, "So far nothing has happened. If it does, I'll let you know."

But Menasco's tip worried him. He was not on as firm legal ground with this piece of land as he had been with Jeffreys or the cattle thief. Certainly, he was complying with the law in every way possible, but the fact remained that he was not eligible to take up land. There was nothing he could do but await developments.

Without mentioning the matter to anyone, he continued to camp every fourth night on the section. One evening as he turned in from the road, he noticed that a good-sized tent had been stretched a little distance from the entrance. From the shadows cast by a lamp inside, he could make out a figure moving around in the tent. As he approached, a man came out. The man not only was big, but also looked muscular and tough. Beyond the tied-back flap, an iron bed, a table, and a rocking chair were plainly visible.

"I don't understand all I see," William said. "Don't you know that you are trespassing on somebody else's property?"

"It ain't yours any more," the big man said, and his confidence matched his size. "Somebody that knows told me about you and said for me to move right in, and that you couldn't do a blamed thing about it."

"Wait and see," William replied. "I'm not going to stand by and watch anyone jump my claim. Remember, I've warned you, and don't get the idea that because I'm just a 'kid,' I'm fooling. I'm giving you till tomorrow to get all this stuff moved off."

With that, he turned his horse, rode out, and jogged back to town.

The following afternoon, William found everything as it had been the night before. Only the owner of the tent was missing. Patiently, but with determination, he tied the contents of the tent, one by one, to his saddlehorn and dragged them into the road. The tent, which had to be unloosed from its stakes and props, was the last to go. After arranging everything in a neat pile, he mounted his horse and rode away.

All that evening and the next day, he stayed in the store, waiting for the repercussion that he felt was inevitable. The man, however, failed to appear. The next time William saw him was through the window of the cab as the train pulled out of town.

"Certainly, you haven't seen him," Menasco explained a few afternoons later, "and I'll tell you why. He was furious when he found out what you had done, and being the sort of man he is, he came to the saloon to get himself into condition to beat the hell out of—as he put it—an 'upstart boy.' The preparation took an hour or so, during which time the sheriff walked in.

"When I saw the sheriff, I thought I'd take advantage of his being there; so I moseyed over to the old drunk and said, 'It might be better for you if you didn't talk so much, and before you start beating the hell out of the Lewis boy, I think you should know a few things. See that big, handsome man over there? He's not only the law around these parts, but he's one of the kid's good friends. Besides, there are plenty of others in town, and if you get smart, they'll make things so hot for you, you'll wish you'd never gotten off your train; so, instead of starting something you can't finish, I suggest you take your things and go back where you came from.'"

CHAPTER XXXIX

During the time William was undergoing trials with tough cattlemen, cow thieves, and claim jumpers, work on the post office had steadily progressed. As soon as it was finished, his father moved in. It did not take long for the new postmaster to discover that he could not run a store and be a servant of the people at the same time. Although both William and his mother had foreseen the difficulties involved in the dual role, they made no attempt to interfere. It was more than apparent that William's father was very pleased with his position as postmaster. Unfortunately, he also enjoyed being a merchant. As a result, both William and his mother were only a little surprised when one evening without preamble, his father broached the subject of selling the store. How would the other members of the family feel about it?

The question confronted William at an unusual period of his life. His one idea since reaching the Panhandle had been to establish a cattle ranch of his own. The thought of being a merchant never once crossed his mind. But the previous years had been rugged ones for a young man of twenty. He was not only physically weary but also closer to discouragement than he had ever been before. From the day he had set out for Carson City to gather Corrigan's steers, everything had been a constant struggle; a struggle against nature; a struggle to maintain his right to pasture his heifers on the public domain; a struggle to hold his herd against cattle thieves; a struggle to hold his land against claim jumpers. Home and town suddenly looked inviting. Maybe, the life of a shopkeeper and tiller of the soil did not have to be as humdrum as he had considered it. Besides, it would solve his father's dilemma, and it would materially help in paying out his mother's cottage. After all, it might be better for him, too. Anyway, he was going to try it. He would buy the store.

Between his father and himself, they arranged that he was to assume the responsibility for all outstanding bills, but that he was to pay his father only for his father's equity in the merchandise. It was an advantage, since it did not make it necessary for him to sell his cattle immediately. By spring many of the heifers would have calved, and that would add to their value.

As soon as he had taken over the business, William started on plans to enlarge the stock and to add a number of items of special appeal to the women customers, such as shoes and millinery. If the store was to be his, it must be the finest emporium in town.

After Christmas, he moved from the room behind the store to his room at home, and his mother was delighted. His father was happily employed in organizing the work routine of the growing post office. The new store was prospering. Altogether, the entire family passed a happy winter.

CHAPTER XL

With the coming of spring 1891, William had no difficulty in disposing of his cattle. Jeffreys, who was as determined as ever to control the lake area, was more than willing to buy them, provided he could have the entire herd. In view of the good price offered, it was a profitable trade, which William could not refuse. As the last young cow and calf were delivered, he felt somehow at a loss. He had done something he had not intended to do, for it had never been his plan to be entirely out of the cattle business even though he had changed from cowboy to merchant.

By the time the cattle were gathered and turned over, it was April, and spring was everywhere. There was an exciting smell of freshness in the air. The plains were sprouting green, and every old cow was followed by a wobbly-legged calf. William did not quite understand his own feelings. For some reason, he hated to return to town after delivering his herd to Jeffreys. He had not realized how good the feel of a saddle on a cutting horse could be, and he did not like the idea of being cooped up indoors while everything out of doors was stirring with new life. It was with a sense of relief that he thought of having to leave shortly for Carson City to gather the final remnant of the Half Circle K herd.

When he reached the high plains the following week, he found the cattle in even better condition than they had been the previous year. After a week of hard work, the rounding was finished, the temporary outfit was paid off, and he and Art Sherrod were on their way to Chicago with the last of the Half Circle K herd.

They stayed in Chicago just long enough for William to do some fall buying for his store and for Art to see a few of the sights in the big city. William's spirits were high during the long train trip home. Things had worked out even better than he had expected. His father had been right in his decision not to go into bankruptcy with the ranch. The cattle had paid themselves out. The only remaining indebtedness was about one thousand dollars due on various bills, the largest amount being Art's unpaid wages. If the store continued to prosper, everything could be settled by the end of the year. Since

Art was planning to continue working for William, there was no hurry about paying him in full. There was plenty to keep him busy in the months to come. The section had to be fenced, and a number of acres put under cultivation. William's father was content in his new occupation, and if the regard in which he was held by the townspeople was any indication, he would retain his appointment as long as he lived. Maybe the difficulties of the past few years were at an end, for a while, anyway.

Instead of going directly home, William and Art went first to Carson City where they had left their own horses as well as the rented *remuda*. It was late afternoon when the train from Chicago arrived, and well into the night before they started for Clarendon. They stopped on the road only long enough to catch a few hours of sleep and to make and drink occasional cups of coffee.

As they drew closer to town, a slight drizzle began to fall. A few miles out, they noticed a glow reflected against the clouds. What could it be? It was unusual to have prairie fires at that season of the year when all the grass was green. They urged their horses on in order to reach town as quickly as possible. It was almost three in the morning when they rode onto the top of the knoll beyond which lay the valley in which Clarendon nestled. Flames were shooting high into the air. The entire place seemed to be burning.

With a shout to Art to look after the horses, William urged his pony on. His first thought was of his parents. Their house, he saw as he raced by, was unharmed and, as yet, out of danger. The fire was several blocks away, with the Wood and Dickson store apparently the center of the conflagration. Without stopping, he rushed on toward his own place of business. As he rounded the corner onto Main Street, he stopped short; not one building on either side of the block next to the depot remained standing. All that was left was part of one wall and piles of damp, smoking debris.

After tying his pony a safe distance away, William returned to the silent crowd of onlookers. After a while, he located his parents who were uninjured but, like the others, too bewildered to give an accurate account of what had happened.

"One person suggested the fire started in the little candy kitchen across the street," exclaimed William's father, "but nobody knows just how. Without water or fire equipment, there was no way to stop it. One building caught fire from the other, and the wind before the rain made things worse. It happened after your mother and I had gone to bed. By the time the noise awakened us and we reached town, flying pieces of wood had set fire to our side of the street. The roof of the store was already ablaze. No one dared to go inside. By then, it was raining steadily but not hard enough to extinguish the flames. When I saw Menasco and a group of friends standing close by, I asked if any attempt had been made to save some of the merchandise before the fire jumped across the street. The gambler said they had thought of it but decided against it. Feeling certain that everything inside was covered by insurance, they hesitated to drag things out into the open where they would not be covered if outside the building."

Although the burning of the store, even with the promise of insurance, was a serious loss, William found the story amusing. "Maybe it was just as well I wasn't in town. I'm not certain I could have taken such good care of myself."

"You will not feel like joking," his father said, "when you hear the rest of it. There is no insurance. The premium came due while you were away. I did not think of it, because, previously, the agent has always given us ample notice. I remembered the moment I saw the flames—too late, unfortunately. I am afraid he has not forgiven me for getting the post office appointment. If that is true and he did what he did intentionally, he could not possibly have chosen a more effective way of punishing me than to bring such disaster on my boy."

For a moment William made no comment. Then he said quietly, "Go on home, Dad. You and mother should be in bed. It's going to be all right. Don't worry. Here is the money for the cattle. Everything's about paid out. I still have to return the horses, so I'll be away for a day or two. When I get back, we'll make new plans."

He walked back to his horse, untied him, mounted, and made himself comfortable in the saddle; then he sat quietly viewing the wreckage before him. As he looked, his life of the last few years passed quickly in review before his eyes. Behind him lay years of hardship, struggle, and, sometimes, bitter experience. Not only had he lost everything he owned except his section of land and his horse, but the money from the sale of his cattle would fall short by several thousand dollars of paying for the merchandise he had purchased in Chicago.

But all this was behind him. The future still lay ahead. After all, the fire might have been a blessing in disguise. Often during his past week on the plains to the north, he had wondered whether he was meant to be a merchant, or if the life of the range was not the life for him. Anyway, the decision had not been his. Fate had made it for him. He remembered his months as an outside man for Rowe. He was not going to be discouraged. He was no longer the boy from Maryland, but a man full-grown and a Texan; no longer the apprentice cowboy, but a seasoned hand. Bad luck could not pursue him always; one day in the future that ranch he wanted so badly would surely be his.

He leaned forward in the saddle, and with a flick of the reins turned his pony toward the river. Ten miles farther on, the Salt Fork trickled lazily along. Beyond the Salt Fork, protected by the breaks of the cap rock, lay the beautiful R.O. Ranch.

The period of apprenticeship was over.

CHAPTER XLI

During the following five years, William continued to work as a top hand for Alfred Rowe. One of his important responsibilities was to deliver the R.O. market cattle safely to the firm of Clay, Robinson and Company of Chicago and Kansas City. It was on one such trip that he was summoned to the office of John Clay, the president.

"So you are young Lewis," Clay said cordially, "the best cattle shipper I know of. I've had my eye on you for some time. It's part of our business to be on the lookout for up-and-coming cattlemen. We are bankers, you know, as well as commission agents. I imagine it won't be too long before you decide to step out for yourself. When you do, let me know. I'll be ready to help."

With Clay's backing, Will—the more dignified William had been dropped, even by the family—began to work for himself. By the time he was thirty, his name was well known and well respected in a wide cattle-raising circle. He bought and sold cattle all over Kansas, New Mexico, and the Panhandle; sometimes in partnership with John Molesworth or Theodore Pyle, and always on leased land.

About 1910 Will leased the famous Spur Ranch. It was before the subdividing of the property began, when the Ranch was still fifty miles long and forty miles wide. It was during the five-year Spur lease that he laid the financial foundation for his success.

The following year he acquired the Shoe Bar Ranch, which had once belonged to Goodnight's brother-in-law Leigh Dyer. And in the fall of the year 1912 he married a Dallas girl. Three daughters and one son, William Jenks Lewis, Jr., were born to this marriage.

Upon the death of Alfred Rowe, who lost his life when the Titanic sank, his widow sold the R.O. Ranch to Will. In 1942 he and Shorty Rorie bought thirty-six thousand acres of the Mill Iron Ranch. In 1947 Will bought his partner's share and established the Flying U Bar Ranch for his daughters.

From the day of the R.O. purchase, the ranch became—in a manner of speaking, since the family never lived on it—the home ranch and a sort of family legend, and Will devoted his entire time to his Texas properties. He ran only Herefords; and the only thoroughbred cattle he ever owned were the young bulls that he purchased annually to assure a calf-crop of superior quality.

He refused the invitation of the government to represent the cattle industry in Washington during World War II. He had no desire for public recognition, and his sole interests were his family and business.

Only once during his long career was he in serious financial difficulty. The Clarendon bank, with which he had long carried his operating loan, sold his notes to a Kansas City banker who preferred the ranch to payment of the borrowed money. Will was not notified of the transfer of the notes until a few weeks before they were due. This occurred during the period following 1929. Money was not available anywhere. After exhausting every possible means, Will was ready to face defeat when the unexpected happened.

From the grasslands of Kansas came a wire from John Huddleston, a banker and rancher; he had just heard of Will's difficulty and had no intention of sitting idly by while an "ornery banker takes the ranch of a man like you."

The ranch was saved.

Will remained vigorous and active until he was well into his seventies. When the end came in 1960, he was still clear of mind and interested in every detail connected with the ranches. During that long lifespan of eighty-nine years, the dignified, soft-spoken boy from Maryland had managed to create a modest but prosperous cattle kingdom consisting of 140,000 acres of land and well over 10,000 head of cattle. The dream he had dreamed at the first branding on the Half Circle K had come true.

All this happened many years ago. The two Williams in whose hearts lay a deep and lasting love of the land are both gone, but cattle still graze the rolling prairies of the R.O., and in spring thousands of white-faced baby calves watch and wait as the mother cows go down to the creek to water.

INDEX

Adair, Cornelia: 146
Adair, John: 15 and n., 146
Adobe Walls: 81, 84, 91
Allen, Parson: 48, 49, 51, 57
Allen Creek: 15, 29, 36, 43, 73, 122, 155, 156, 175
Amarillo: 130
antelope: 101, 102–103
Arapaho Indians: 80
Ashley, Hon. John Majoribanks: 31
Ashley, Hon. Percival: 31
atacosa: 98–99

barbed wire: xv
Bar O Ranch: 16, 53
B. H. White and Company: described, 20, 49, 127; location of, 41; gun raffle at, 49–51; robbery of, 142–145; mentioned, 35
Birl (Negro boy): at branding, 51, 53; story of, 55–57; at church, 59; puppy given to, 67; role of, with ranch hands, 70, 71, 73, 82; as William's friend, 71; made to ride bronc, 72–73; fear of horses of, 77
Blaylock, Don: 54
blizzard: of 1886, 67–68; of 1888, 136–138; of 1890, 161
Boggy Creek: 15, 73–74, 122, 123, 126
Boney (cook): 73, 81, 84, 107, 120
boots: importance of, 108 and n.
Borscher, Mr.: 145, 149
branding: 51–52, 53
broncbusting: 54, 72, 78, 86–87, 88 and n., 89, 90–94

Brown, Barr: 54
Browning, James U. (judge): 115
Brush, J. H.: 128–130, 150, 153
Buchanan, Dave: 54
Buck (pony): 89, 90
Buck Creek: 14, 111
buffalo hunting: xv, 11, 83
Bull-cob Mountain: 36
Bushey Creek: 29, 58

Canadian River: 31, 39, 65, 74, 77, 80, 83, 85, 92, 95, 147
cap rock: 16, 68, 139, 182
Carhart, Lewis Henry: establishes Quarter Circle Heart Ranch, 3, 117–118; ends ranching role, 94, 127; mentioned, 25, 40, 139 n.
Carroll Creek: 14, 29, 36, 43, 53, 91, 92
Carson City: 133, 162, 174, 175, 180
Carson County: 15 n.
cattle raising: 117, 118, 146
cattle rustling: xiii, 167–172, 174
Chamberlain, Ben: 21, 139, 166, 174–175
Cheyenne Indians: 80
Chicago: 130, 165
Civil War: 32
Clarendon, Christian Colony of: establishment of, 3; William's trip to, 9–14, 19; description of, 21; changes in, 40, 124, 127; entertainment in, 59, 75; leasing trial in, 113–117; mentioned, xii, 11, 18, 22, 36, 37, 44, 47, 50, 70, 112

Clarendon (new town): described, 124; building of, 124, 130–133, 145; character of settlers of, 131, 132–133
Clay, John: 182
Collingsworth County: 169
Colorado: 3
Comanche Indians: 11, 83–84, 91
Cooper, W. A. (Methodist minister): helps unpack, 23–24; and church activities, 24, 25, 59, 67; marries Katie, 166; Methodism of, 145–146
Corbett, Mr. (bootmaker): 28, 58, 59, 135
Corrigan, Thomas: 18 and n., 129, 152, 161
cowboy: art of, 11–12, 78. SEE ALSO Lewis, William Jenks; broncbusting
Cummins, Mr. (cowboy): 91–95

Diamond F Ranch: 15 and n.
Doan's Crossing: xv, 11
Dodge City: 139 n.
Donley County: 18, 31, 64, 116
Dyer, Leigh: 32, 183

Eagle Hill: 22
enclosure: 18, 146–147
Enclosure Act: 65–66, 123
escarpment: 80

farmers: threat of, to ranchers, 117, 146
fire: threat of, 119; William fights prairie, 119–122; at William's store, 180–182
Fort Elliott: 22
Fort Sill: 83
Fort Sumner: 74, 104–105, 107
Fort Worth: 3, 5
Fort Worth and Denver Railroad: 32, 124, 127, 130, 132, 146
Francklyn Land and Cattle Company: 15 n., 118
free grass: era of, xv, 146–148, 151, 174; importance of, to Half Circle K, 16, 17; discussed, 63; rounding on, 100
Freeman, Billy: 54, 78
Frey, Mr. (rustler): 169–172
frontier: myth of, xi–xii; tales of, 10–12, 35–36, 62–63; problems of, 64

gambling: 8, 32, 40, 150
Gatherin, Mr. (muleteer): 42, 47–48, 136
Gentry, Al: 31, 141–144
Gentry, Sella: 67
Goodnight, Charles: to Panhandle, 3; J. A. Ranch of, 15 and n.; Koogle works for, 16; descriptions of, 31, 147, 148; William's family visits, 60–63; frontier stories of, 62–63, 64; on leasing, 63, 66; on free grass, 63, 146–148; and Adair's death, 146; political contacts of, 147; and Koogle, 147–148; buys Half Circle K, 150–152, 153, 154–159; and William, 154–160; mentioned, xiii
Goodnight, Mollie: 31, 160
Gormley, Pat: 54
Gray County: 15 n.
Greer County: 15 n.
Groom, B. B.: 15 n., 117–118
Groom, Harry: 15 n.
gun slinger: xiii
Gunter and Munson: 31

Half Circle K Ranch: description of, 17; brand of, 18, 52; problems of, 68, 119, 128–130; good season of, 150; sale of, 150–152, 154, 174; mentioned 127, 146, 184. SEE ALSO Lewis, William Jenks
Harrold: description of, 6, 8; William at, 6–7; mentioned, 22, 36, 49, 133
Hitson, Sam: 54, 82, 83, 111
Holden, Bill: 28
hoodlum: described, 35
Houston, Temple: 147
Huddleston, John: 184
Hutchinson County: 15 n.

Indians: as horse thieves, xiii, 80; subjugation of, xv; Doan's crossing raid of, 11; threat of, 22, 43, 80; demand buffalo, 61–62; demand cow, 80–81
Indian Territory: 3, 13, 62, 74

J. A. Ranch: 15 and n., 16, 146
J. B. cattle: 18
jerky: 10, 12, 60
Jefferson, Em: 12, 19, 131, 133, 135, 138
Jefferson, Harry: 136, 138

Jefferson, Ralph: description of, 12, 16; as partner in Half Circle K, 14, 128; as postmaster, 19, 125; stores of, 127, 130–131, 136; drinking habits of, 135, 136, 138, 148–149; to Washington, D.C., 149; mentioned, 22, 25, 133
Jeffreys, Mr. (rancher): 167–169, 176, 179
Johnson, Ed: 54

Kansas: 11
Kelly Creek: 14
Kilfoil, Mr. (buffalo-bone hunter): 45
Kiowa: 11
Koogle, Bill: ambitions of, xii; Satterwhite on, 11; background of, 14, 16 and n.; investments of, 14, 16–17, 18; and ranch, 17, 25, 26, 40 and n., 65, 68, 147; debt of, to Brush, 18–19, 129; visits of, to Clarendon, 27; odd behavior of, 40 and n., 75, 128, 150; on Birl, 57; and Enclosure Act, 65, 123; competence of, questioned, 94; business practices of, 129; drinking habits of, 136, 150; to Mexico, 151; mentioned, 127, 152 n., 161
Koogle, Carrie: house for, 17; and ranch, 40; child of, 66, 67; to Kansas City, 68, 152; obligations to, 162

leasing: Goodnight on, 63, 66; violation of laws for, 113; trial, 113–117; laws on, 174
Lewis, Charles (William's father): trip of, to Panhandle, xv, 5, 7; investments of, 14; background of, 16; activities of, in Clarendon, 19–20, 22–25; reaction of, to West, 21, 40; and cattle business, 25, 53, 68, 76; merchant ventures of, 41, 124–125, 128, 130, 138; and Birl's story, 57; in new Clarendon, 137, 138, 150; banking arrangements of, 133; and post office, 138, 146, 172, 177; sells Half Circle K to Goodnight, 150–152, 153; obligations of, 161–162, 165; and store fire, 181
Lewis, Charles, Jr.: 5 n.
Lewis, Hallie Koogle (William's mother): trip of, to Panhandle, xv, 5, 7–8; and jerky, 10; on Ralph Jefferson, 12; life of, in Clarendon, 21, 22, 24, 25, 26, 131, 152; on William, 112, 142; pioneer qualities of, 137
Lewis, Katie (William's sister): trip of, to Panhandle, 5; on picnic, 12; in Clarendon, 25; job of, 138; and Ben Chamberlain, 139, 166
Lewis, William Jenks: to Panhandle, xii, xv, 3, 5–14; love of plains of, xii, 39, 63, 78, 84; animosity of Red Williams toward, xiii, 69, 70, 71, 78–79, 84; jobs of, at R. O. Ranch, xiii, 112, 173, 174; buys R. O. Ranch, xiii, 183; frontier stories told to, 10–12, 35–36, 62–64; on Ralph Jefferson, 12–13; life of, in Clarendon, 19–20, 21, 22, 25–28, 31–33, 49–51, 58, 59, 60–63, 66, 67–68, 135–136; at furniture unpacking, 22–25; and Tex, 26, 28–29, 69, 82–83; surveying job of, 33, 34–35, 37–38, 39–40; and rattlers, 38, 61, 101–103; and mustangs, 38; and mules, 39, 42, 43–48; assistance of, in father's stores, 41–42, 125, 131–135, 139, 140, 178; ambitions of, 48, 139–140, 178; investments of, 51, 57, 123, 126, 166–167, 174–175; and blizzards, 68, 137; and roundups, 69, 75, 77, 80, 86, 89, 91–94, 107–112, 127, 130, 159, 162–165; and Birl, 53, 55–57, 70, 71; and Half Circle K, 53, 71, 73, 146, 179; broncbusting of, 78, 86–87, 88 and n., 89–94; as guard, 81–83, 89; defies Red, 85, 95–96; Red friendly to, 87, 106, 108, 111, 139, 159 and n.; ponies of, 88, 89, 90, 92, 121–122; maturing of, 97, 112, 142; and antelope, 101–103; at Fort Sumner, 105–106; on lobo chase, 110–111; and fires, 119–122, 180–182; and bad check incident, 125–126, 140–142; and robbery of tent store, 133–135; transactions of, with Goodnight, 154–159, 160; threat to land of, 175–177; adult life of, 182–184; death of, 184
Lewis, William Jenks, Jr.: 183, 184
Lewis, Willie Newbury: xii, xiii, 183
line rider: 18

lobo: 109, 110–111, 119
Lyle Dave: 78–79, 85

McClelland, Bruce: 31
McClelland, Stanhope: 31
McClelland Creek: 15, 77, 119, 122
McKinney, Al: 94
Maryland: xii, 3, 6, 11, 19, 21, 29, 41, 184
maverick: 79, 154
Menasco, Bill: background of, 42; as William's friend, 42, 47–48, 136, 141; mentioned, 175, 177
mesquite: 74
Methodism: 3, 145–146
Mexican cowboy: background of, 54–55; rescues Birl, 73; death of 108–109
Mobeetie: 22
Murdock, Judge: 94
Murdock, Will: 27, 43, 48–51, 58–59
mustang: 38, 80

nester: xvi; SEE ALSO farmer
New Mexico: 3, 62, 67, 104
New York and Texas Land Company: 15 n.

Oklahoma. SEE Indian Territory

Palo Duro Canyon: 3, 100, 109
Palo Duro Creek: 100
Panhandle: violence of, xi–xii; William's family arrives in, xv, 3, 5–14; descriptions of, 3, 60, 64, 74, 147; blizzards of, 67–68, 136–138, 161; customs of, 114; settlement of, 116; economy of, 117, 118; mentioned, 31, 65 n. SEE ALSO Clarendon, Christian Colony of; Clarendon (newtown)
Parker, Quanah: 11, 91
Parks, Mr. (surveyor): 33, 35, 37, 38–40
Parks, Vashti: 32, 67
Patchin, Fred (Bar O Kid): as broncbuster, 54, 72, 87, 90; and Birl, 73; saves Red, 97; and antelope, 101; and lobo incident, 110–111; mentioned, 53, 163
Pease River: 10
Phillips, Clint: 54

plains: description of, 10, 36, 84, 99–100; Great, 14–15, 30; North, 16, 80
Pony (William's pony): 88, 92, 121–122
post office: 19, 41, 131. SEE ALSO Lewis, Charles
Prairie Dog Fork: 3, 13, 100, 109

Quarter Circle Heart Ranch: established by Carhart, 3, 117; losses of, 68; on roundup, 77, 91, 94; to receiver, 127, 128; mentioned, 15, 27, 36, 43, 49
quickie: 89
Quitaque Ranch: 146, 152

railroads: 32. SEE ALSO under individual railroads
ranchers: 117, 118, 146
rattlesnake: danger of, 30, 109; diamondback, kills cowboy, 102–104, 103 n.
Rawhide Creek: 15
Record Creek: 15
Red River: 3, 11, 77, 100, 109, 124, 146
remuda: described, 51, 77; during storm, 107; mentioned, 72, 78, 80, 86, 180
Rhoderick, Bernie: 27, 126, 132
Roberts County: 15 n.
Rockingchair Ranch: 31, 111, 169
R. O. Ranch: William top hand of, xiii; William owner of, xiii, 183; on roundup, 77; described, 139–140; mentioned, 31, 111, 167, 169, 170, 172, 182, 184
Rosenfield, Morris (Rosie): and B. H. White and Company, 20, 127, 142–145; and William, 20, 28, 34–35, 48; and William's family, 22, 128–130; activities of, 24, 49–51; on lease trial, 114; mentioned, xv
Ross, Bill (bullwhacker): 20, 22
roundup: organization of, described, 74–75; festivities before, 76; activities during, 77, 79, 80–85, 86, 104; thunderstorm during, 107–109; to liquidate Half Circle K, 159, 173–174. SEE ALSO Lewis, William Jenks
Rowe, Alfred: at open house, 31; and

William, 112, 169, 170, 182; background of, 139 and n.
Rowe, Bernard: 139 n.
Rowe, Vincent: 139 n.
Roxy, Mr. (stagedriver): 44
Rustler's Creek: 13

Sacra and Sugg Ranch: 15, 16, 53
St. Louis, Missouri: 146
Sales Act Amendment of 1887 (Seven Section Act): 65 and n., 147
Salt Fork: located, 3, 21; importance of, to Half Circle K, 17; mentioned, 14, 16, 74, 77, 135, 182
Satterwhite, Mr. (muleteer): 10–12, 13, 58
Sherman, Texas: 3
Sherrod, Art: saves Red, 97; and William, 100–101, 120–121, 159, 163, 164; and lobo incident, 110–111; mentioned, 53, 173, 179, 180
Shoe Bar Ranch: 183
Skillet Creek: 112, 139 n.
Southern Kansas Railroad: 32, 130
South Texas: 49, 52
Spur Ranch: 129, 183
Stanton, Rev. Mr.: 21
Stocking, Dr.: 27 and n., 145
surveying: 37–38. SEE ALSO Lewis, William Jenks

Tabor, Mr.: 29, 31
Tabor, Mrs.: 29, 31
Tandy, Mr. (stockman): 18, 51, 52–53, 129
tapadero: defined, xiii, 55
Tascosa: 36, 44, 91, 98, 169
Tex (William's pony): given to William, 26; as William's companion, 29, 48, 69; death of, 82–83; mentioned, 43
Tierra Blanca Creek: 100
trail driving: described, 92
Tyler, Texas: 55

unlocated land: defined, 17
Utes: 36

vara: defined, 37

Wakefield, Mr. (cowboy): 50
Washington, D. C.: 5 n., 12, 84, 149
Wells-Fargo Express: 143
White, B. H. (judge): activities of, 20, 128–130; open house of, 31–33; description of, 31–32; on railroads, 32; on lease trial, 114
White, Lottie: 31
White Deer Lands: 15 n.
White Fish property: 139 n.
Wichita Falls: 6
Williams, Red: character of, xii, 53, 85, 86; animosity of, to William, xiii, 69–70, 71, 78, 79, 84; background of, 69–70; and Birl, 71, 72–73; and Indians, 81; and roundup, 85, 95–97, 100, 104–105; friendliness of, to William, 87, 106, 108, 111, 139, 159 and n.; and lobo incident, 110–111; and Goodnight, 154
Willis, Frank, Sr. (judge): 115, 116, 117 n.
Wood and Dickson: 124, 127, 130, 143
Woodman, W. H. (judge): 115

XIT Ranch: 16, 100